book
of ideas

A journal of creative direction
and graphic design

Radim Malinic

Volume 1

Brand Nu®

First published in the United Kingdom in 2016
by Brand Nu Limited, www.brandnu.co.uk

Book of Ideas - A journal of creative direction
and graphic design ©2016 Radim Malinic

4 5 6 7 8 9 10 / 22 21 20 19 18

Written and designed by Radim Malinic
Copyediting by Emily Gosling and Anne Wollenberg

All showcase images and photos by
©Brand Nu® unless otherwise stated.

British Library Cataloguing-in-Publication Data
A catalogue record for this book is available
from the British Library

ISBN 978-0-9935400-0-4

Proudly printed and bound in
England by Taylor Bloxham

350gsm GalerieArt Satin - FSC Mix
100gsm UPM Fine Offset - FSC Mix

To find out more about this publication or the author,
please visit brandnu.co.uk or bookofideas.co.uk

MIX
Paper from
responsible sources
FSC® C022127
FSC
www.fsc.org

BOOK OF IDEAS / THIS IS MY JOURNAL OF CREATIVE DIRECTION AND GRAPHIC DESIGN; A COLLECTION OF THOUGHTS, MUSINGS, AND OBSERVATIONS FROM MY UPS AND DOWNS IN THE CREATIVE INDUSTRY. IT'S ABOUT HOW THE WORLD OUTSIDE INFLUENCES THE CREATIVITY INSIDE; AND HOW IT INSPIRES US, TEACHES US AND MAKES US CREATE BETTER WORK /

BY RADIM MALINIC

Volume 1

BOOK OF IDEAS / CONTENTS

/ WORK

/ CREATIVITY

/ MIND

Volume 1

BOOK OF IDEAS /
INTRODUCTION

It's now ten years since I decided to go it alone in pursuit of making the best creative work I can. I left behind the tempting reliability of a monthly salary and fixed working hours in favour of the unknown. If I hadn't done so, you wouldn't be holding this book in your hands. I needed to go and discover everything for myself, and I had to make a lot of mistakes doing so. I needed to write my own story.

I started thinking about this book concept a few years ago as a graphic designer, and I finished it as a creative director. I got there by saying yes to pretty much every opportunity I thought I could either learn from or do a good job at. I'm curious about everything. Thanks to my clients, who I call collaborators, I have learned about so many aspects of the making process. All of this happened while creating the work that I love.

The title of this book was decided a long time ago - before I even wrote the list of chapters. For a long time, I was mostly seduced by pretty visual eye candy: I used to only think in colour and image aesthetics. Then, I got to a point where I found myself needing one more thing - a reason. This collection of my work has been chosen from the last few years of searching for purpose and reasons.

Every chapter in this book is a memo from the diary I never had. It shows there's been a cognitive shift: I stopped talking over people and started listening. I wanted to better understand the questions. When I did, I realised I needed extra skills and knowledge to take me further in my career. It was time to learn in order to grow.

So this is it. This is my book of ideas - a journal of stories, musings, thoughts, and observations. I hope there's something in this book that will inspire you.

THE ART OF ASKING QUESTIONS

No one has ever looked stupid for asking questions and no one ever will. Being able to get to the heart of any task is the key to being good at what you do, regardless of your profession.

Asking questions should be simple, but it can also be an art form that will help you and your clients. Just because somebody tells us what they want, it doesn't mean that it's what they actually need.

Our face-to-face conversations are mostly communicated non-verbally. Each tiny gesture helps to explain things. The more distant and impersonal our conversations, the more information we lose.

Knowing all this, why do we think that a short client email with basic information means full knowledge of the commission? When you think of a client brief in a Word document, you shouldn't accept at face-value that all the information you need is there. Clients are not often designers themselves, so never take a project brief for granted.

When somebody says they want to use blue, it doesn't always mean the blue that you can visualise. There are thousands of shades of blue - what is it that they actually want? This is where the art of asking questions is vital.

We all think we want something specific until somebody points out that, in fact, we are after something else. Even the most confident and assured client has never thought of absolutely everything. No-one has.

Design Matters
Computer Arts Magazine
typography

DESIGN
MATTERS

LOOKING FOR REASONS

Every design problem comes with a solution. Although it's usually hidden, it's there, waiting to be discovered. You might find it in a day or a week, but the key is in understanding the meaning of the question.

Today, we're surrounded by choices. Things can be any colour, any shape or any size. Most of these choices can be done with the click of a button, changing a plate or by using a different material. The key to success is to search and combine the most fitting options together.

It takes an elevated view of the situation to see all sides of the problem. It's all too easy to start fixing an issue on one side when the others are in greater need of attention.

If you don't understand the thing you're designing for, you're only creating work for yourself with the hope that you might get lucky and somebody will sign it off before you can run away.

Place yourself in the shoes of the user and observe the inner workings of the situation or product. Only then can you identify the problems, and go on to find the answers.

The style you add to a design is what demonstrates your individual voice, but the substance has to stay the same. Style acts as the coating for an inner working engine, like the paintwork of a car. While the coating might get scratched or repainted, the engine will keep moving forward as normal.

Learn how to build engines.

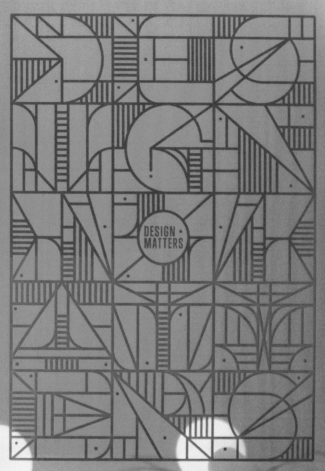

WORK FOR YOUR SOUL /
THE ART OF CHOOSING CLIENTS

If you do unenjoyable work for unappreciative people
you will end up doing more of the same for someone else.
You can get caught up in a cycle of work that is no good
to anyone. This is why choosing the right clients really matters.

When it comes to making decisions about new work and clients,
there are a few simple questions which you should ask yourself
in the following order:

Can you do your best work on this project?
Will you get on with these people?
Is this something you believe in?
Is the budget realistic?
Would you be happy to do this work again?

Whatever I do, I want it to be the best piece of work in my portfolio.
I don't believe in just doing mechanical work with no meaning. Creative
work should be good for the soul. If I'm making a difference by helping
a good cause or getting a new start-up off the ground then for me the
budget is the least important thing.

Project briefs can be tempting. They can promise a lot, but they don't
always deliver as much as they claim. A big household brand is pretty
much certain to get anyone they want as designers are queuing to tick
off names on their 'dream client' list. For these clients, it's easy.

Budgets can be even more tempting. It is easy to be seduced
by big numbers, which can make your judgement fuzzy for
a moment. However, when the project seems too good to
be true, it pretty much always is.

There's no easy way to get it right all the time. Choosing clients
should be about the opportunities that will keep you on the
right track. Just choose the work you want to do.

Work for your soul and success will follow.

**Haywire Saint
album artwork**
digital illustration

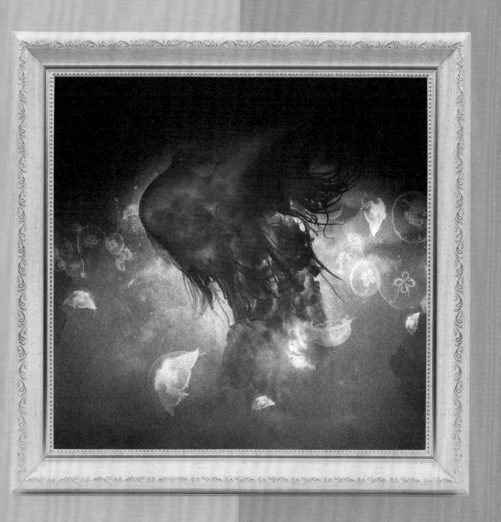

Ark
Ark by Night
invitation design

you are invited to join us at

ARK BY NIGHT

· WEDNESDAY 4 NOVEMBER 2015 ·

TUESDAY 3 NOVEMBER
6.15pm
Ark Globe Academy
Harper Road
London
SE1 6AG

Experience
another world...

Timings
Please arrive promptly at 6.15pm; a valet parking
service will be available. Your journey will begin at
6.45pm and an informal supper will follow at 8pm.
We expect the evening to finish by 10pm.

Dress
Dress comfortably and come prepared
for something a little different

RSVP
Eleanor.Gall@arkonline.org or 020 3116 6385

Ark

CLIENT /
COLLABORATOR

I use the word client far too often – in conversations,
interviews or even in this book. The term client can feel cold,
or even just a bit weird, especially given the setting of intricate
creative work. So when I am working with a client I hardly ever
see them that way. To me, a 'client' is a 'collaborator'. We work
together towards a common goal, with our different skillsets
and knowledge complementing each other. We are a
collaborative project team.

This simple cognitive shift helps me to see people and their
projects in another unique way. The client/collaborator should
not be someone we only speak to at the beginning and the
end of the process. Any creative project should be about the
crossover of worlds that can benefit from knowing a lot more
about each other. In situations like these, everyone will grow as
a professional, picking up information and knowledge to help
with future work. We help to get the best out of each other.

In sport, the best teams have a specialist for every position on
the field and they pull together to win the game. In business,
the best-performing teams are the ones where skillsets
compliment each other. No one person is the best at everything.

Collaboration should not be seen as a compromise. Good
teamwork is about listening to every single voice in the group
before you find the best logical outcome. Of course, this is not
an easy process, but in most projects, people come together
and look for ways to do something amazing together. This is
the true spirit of collaboration.

Whatever you call your client/collaborator to others, always
think of them as the people on your side. That's how you win.

MediaMath

**X-Pop Artist bluetooth speakers
for X-Dream & Wowzr**
vector illustration

radim malinic

X-Pop
PLAY
vector illustration

BUILDING TRUST AND KEEPING IT

There are two vital ingredients for great work - a killer idea and somebody who will put their faith in it. No great project was ever produced without the client putting their trust in creative hands. You can promise the earth but no-one will commission it unless they believe in you.

In our lives and relationships, trust enables us to live freely. In the creative and business world, trust has to be earned to exist. When a product breaks too soon or easily, we don't buy it again. We don't want to waste our money and energy.

When you start working on a new account or project, there's a slim chance you'll hit gold right away. It's likely you'll hit a few dead ends, and you might find it very hard to get a radical yet exciting idea past the decision-makers. The back and forth process can feel endless and frustrating. Then, all of a sudden, the message gets through. The work is getting signed off. People are happy once again.

There was no shift in the quality of the ideas - they have been the same all along. It's only that now, the decision-makers believe in what you've got. They trust their investment isn't going to waste. You made them believe that what you've got is going to be a success.

It doesn't matter if you are a freelancer or a multi-national agency, there are times when you will have to establish the solid foundations of a working relationship. No-one ever opens their chequebook without worrying about the possible risks. When you have your client's trust, try to never to lose it. It's very hard to earn it back.

RALEIGH RITCHIE & SOUNWAVE

NEVER SAY DIE

GET THE WORK YOU WANT

Getting new client work can seem like a dark art. Getting the right type of work can seem even more difficult. There are many different ways of getting hold of projects and each type of creative outfit employs a different tactic.

New projects can be won in pitches, they can be agreed over lunch with a long-term contact, or while the new business people and agents cold-call the earth. Some work is done for the love of the craft, some for money to keep the studio going. The first type of project usually goes in the portfolio - the second type gets hidden and forgotten.

When prospective clients start looking for a creative, the process usually begins in one of three places: a Google search, word of mouth recommendation or first-hand experience with the work you have created. The client will browse sites, compile a shortlist, then proceed with an email enquiry.

From the client perspective, this should be straightforward. The client emails five people selected from their online portfolios. Those five emails will be met with as many different responses. One or two emails won't get answered for a few days, the third person will quote rather cheaply, the fourth person will send a quote which is double that. The last person will analyse the email and think about the project and what value they can add. Is it suitable for them? Is it playing to their strengths? Can they do a great job? They will pick up the phone and call the sender back to find out more. Although their quote might end up the most expensive, they are the most likely to get the job.

It is so easy to see enquiries as passing traffic. If clients take the time to make the initial contact, it's silly to simply reply with a robotic answer. Even if the current enquiry isn't fully right for you, stay in touch.

No email will ever beat a phone call. Regardless of the business size, the key is to be personable and to show willing to turn the client's brief into a success. People will buy into your enthusiasm more than your Photoshop skills.

THE ART OF
SELF-PROMOTION

The creative industry serves to create work that promotes businesses and products. So why are so many creatives so bad at promoting themselves? And why do designers spend so much energy on promoting themselves to other designers and not real clients?

There are scores of promo prints being sent to advertising art buyers who are inundated with these things, yet there's many a marketing manager desperately looking for someone to help with a project.

Then there are mass portfolio websites. They are brimming with incredible talent and millions of projects. But if directory websites worked so well, why are the majority of people always scrambling for work? Far too many people see them as the holy grail.

When it comes to building a showcase portfolio website, it's wrong to assume images alone will do the talking. The fewer words there are, the fewer people will find the site through a Google search. If you're a freelancer or a small business, you have to have a fully functioning website with words to improve SEO. You have to help people to find you.

Creatives need to realise that everyone is a potential client. You can start by walking down your local high street and finding a business, shop or restaurant with a logo, menu or website that needs some attention. Step in and offer your services. Help that business to grow and they will help your career in return. Grow slowly upwards through work for real clients.

**Birger Jarl
Summer**
event branding

BIRGER JARL

HERE
COMES
SUMMER

SOMMARENS
BÄSTA NÖJE

ÖPPETIDER
Fredagar 22.30–03.00
Lördagar 22.30–03.00

bj

BIRGERJARL
Nedre Slottsgatan 3
753 09 Uppsala

www.birgerjarl.nu

/14

CONTACT
Telefon: 018-13 50 00
Fax: 018-13 00 12

info@birgerjarl.nu

Birger Jarl
Winter
event branding

BIRGER JARL
HERE
COMES
WINTER

bj   /14

OPPETIDER
Fredagar 22.00-03.00
Lördagar 22.00-03.00

BIRGER JARL
Nedre Slottsgatan 7
753 09 Uppsala

www.birgerjarl.nu

CONTACT
Telefon 018 13 60 00
Fax 018 13 60 12

info@birgerjarl.nu

NO AGENT IS A MAGICIAN

Agents: those elusive and mysterious people with the black notebook of inexhaustible contacts that will guarantee you long-term career success. Listening to the chatter at any creative gathering, conference or art school design class, it seems that majority of people would like to have an agent. They usually see them as the answer to all their problems - getting work, being noticed in the industry and not worrying about the future.

Unless you already have talent or skill, no agent will ever be the answer to a non-existent career. Agents can only amplify the good you already have. They can help you find the chart-topping hit in you, but they can't teach you to sing.

An agent is a creatively-minded sales person who builds their business on trading your creativity as a commodity. You'll get to sign on the dotted line either for your talent or your style. Rarely is it a combination of both.

If there is demand for your style, the price of your work can go up. But as with any supply and demand situation, others can start trading off the same thing, and your style can soon seem outdated.

But if your talent is the focus of interest, an agent could be the right enabler to provide new leads where you can generate something fresh every time. Just like actors who can play lead roles in different movie genres, you can adapt your talent and deliver a killer performance. Sadly, this kind of scenario is a lot less common. A style is quicker to sell.

Everyone wants an agent, but not everyone needs one.

**Mystery Box
x Brand Nu VR**
vector illustration
+ packaging

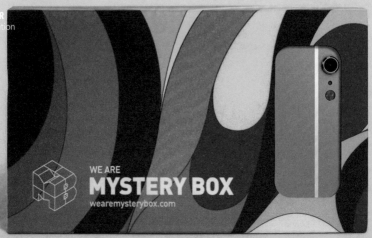

WE ARE
MYSTERY BOX
wearemysterybox.com

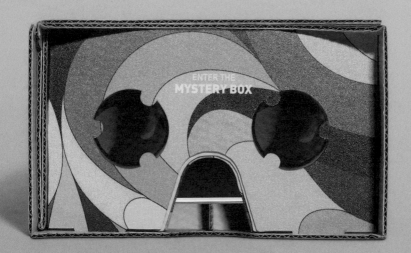

IF IT LOOKS EASY, IT NEVER IS

When you least expect it, a special kind of project brief lands in your inbox. It seems close to perfection. For once you feel you might not have to go through hoops to get your voice heard. You begin to think you can just concentrate on doing a great job. The time has come for your dream project.

That's how you tend to think when your mind is cloudy with excitement and you can't believe how lucky you are. Your cognitive capacity is quite limited at this moment. You can easily trick yourself into a false sense of security.

I've always found that if something looks easy to do, it hardly ever is. Every single time.

Creative briefs can be tricky beasts. They might say one thing and mean something totally different. Even how you read into them can be misleading. So when your dream job lands in your inbox, treat it like an alien. Take a few steps back and keep looking at it. Does it really look so great? What's the catch?

When you keep asking questions and interrogating their answers, a dream outcome becomes more likely. It should never be easy. When you're not challenged, you're not likely to create brilliance.

Even if something looks like it was easy to create, it's usually the result of really hard work.

**Blistex packaging refresh
w/ Bray Leino**
digital illustration

Blistex

Soothing
Splash™
REFRESHING

Lip-loving rollerball
drenches lips with
moisture while Jojoba,
Aloe Vera and Menthol
condition, refresh and
perk up your pout.
Feel the freshness!

SPF 15

Blistex

MedPlus™
Cherry
Berry
FRUITY FIXER

A burst of berries with
comforting Camphor,
Beeswax and Cocoa
Butter to deal with dryness
and leave lips gorgeously
juicy. Works a treat!

SPF 15

Blistex

NEW

Raspberry
Lemonade
Blast™
ZINGY

Wake up lacklustre lips
with a blast of fruit flavour
and moisturising Jojoba,
and Vitamins C & E for
a more deliciously
kissable pout. Yum!

SPF 15

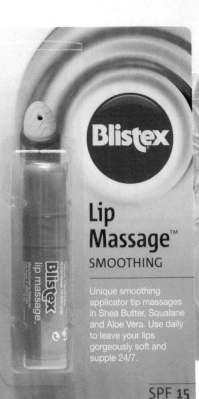

Blistex

Intensive Moisturiser
HYDRATING

A long-lasting daily hydration fix for lips. With Shea Butter, Camphor and Allantoin to condition, perfect and protect deep down.

SPF 10

Blistex

Lip Massage™
SMOOTHING

Unique smoothing applicator tip massages in Shea Butter, Squalane and Aloe Vera. Use daily to leave your lips gorgeously soft and supple 24/7.

SPF 15

Blistex

Daily Lip Condition
CARING

Keep your lips looking luscious and lovely. Cond and moisturise every day with nurturing Olive Grape Seed Oil and Aloe Vera.

SPF

La Tordera
Future to Grow
bottle redesign pitch

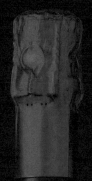

La Tordera

Alné

PROSECCO SMILLESIMATO
TREVISO DOC

La Tordera

Brunei

VALDOBBIADENE DOCG
PROSECCO SUPERIORE

Brut

**Malibu by
Brand Nu**
custom bottle graphics

BEATING THE CREATIVE BLOCK

Every once in a while, everyone in the creative industry will wrestle with the dreaded creative block. No one is immune to that moment where you feel like giving up and planning for a new career through pure frustration in that moment.

So when you have to have an idea right here, right now, how do you win the fight and come up with the right solution?

First, stop panicking - take a step back and get a clear view of what's going on. You need to free up some space to think, so take a few deep breaths without worrying about the looming deadline. Go for a run or go for lunch. Just get out of your studio when you can.

You need to get another perspective. No project was ever solved by putting in extra hours of directionless labour.

To get to where you need to be, use successful projects as reference points and look for the 'why' instead of 'how' the project succeeded. Understanding another person's thought process can help you immensely. Every great project carries a strong idea, regardless of its colour, typeface, finish or render. It could help you understand where to go next.

Whatever you think you are meant to be doing, do the opposite. Put together a mood board of working samples, collect images in a new Pinterest board, pick up a pencil and draw, or write down anything that comes into your mind. The key is in picking up momentum and collecting fragments to help you form a fitting answer to your problem.

Next time, you can start with these problem solving tools right from the start.

Sprite Vietnam
w/ Google Labs London
digital illustration + packaging

Birger Jarl
'We own the night'
staff apparel design

HEY!
CAN I
HELP
YOU?

bj

STAFF

BIRGER JARL
Nedre Slottsgatan 3
753 09 Uppsala

www.birgerjarl.nu

WE OWN
THE NIGHT

HEY!
CAN I
HELP
YOU?

W S E
O T WN
A T H
E F N
bj I G F
HT

BIRGERJARL
Nedre Slottsgatan 3
753 09 Uppsala

www.birgerjarl.nu

CONTACT
Telefon: 018-13 50 00
Fax: 018-13 00 12

info@birgerjarl.nu

TAKING PRIDE IN YOUR WORK

During the course of any career, we're likely to be faced with many pieces of 'helpful' advice. Colleagues, friends, and bosses will all want to furnish you with their wisdom. Inevitably, there's going to be good and bad advice, both in plentiful supply.

Before I landed my first graphic design job, I was an assistant in a high street print shop. It was the place where you would go to get a custom 'Happy Birthday' t-shirt printed for a friend or relative. Nonetheless, the place was meant to be supplying creative solutions. Clearly, this shop wasn't about ground breaking, D&AD award-winning work, but surely it was meant to be good enough to grow its reputation for repeat custom? Yet to my surprise I was soon told to lower my ambition as the prices charged didn't warrant 'good design'. "Don't make it look good, they didn't pay enough for it," is an exact quote. I found it as preposterous that day as I do today. I want to enjoy my work regardless of the budget.

We make decisions for many reasons. Money should never be the deciding factor of how good your work can be. We should take pride in our work.

In today's creative industry, first impressions matter more than ever – so I wish more people really cared about the opportunities they are given. Being a designer is not about being a superstar in the making. It's about the chance to change the world one step at a time, even if that step is just a poster, magazine cover or branding project. Go and seize the opportunity and show the world how good you really are.

Make it look the best you can, regardless of the budget.

Foals
Holy Fire Tour
T-shirt design pitch

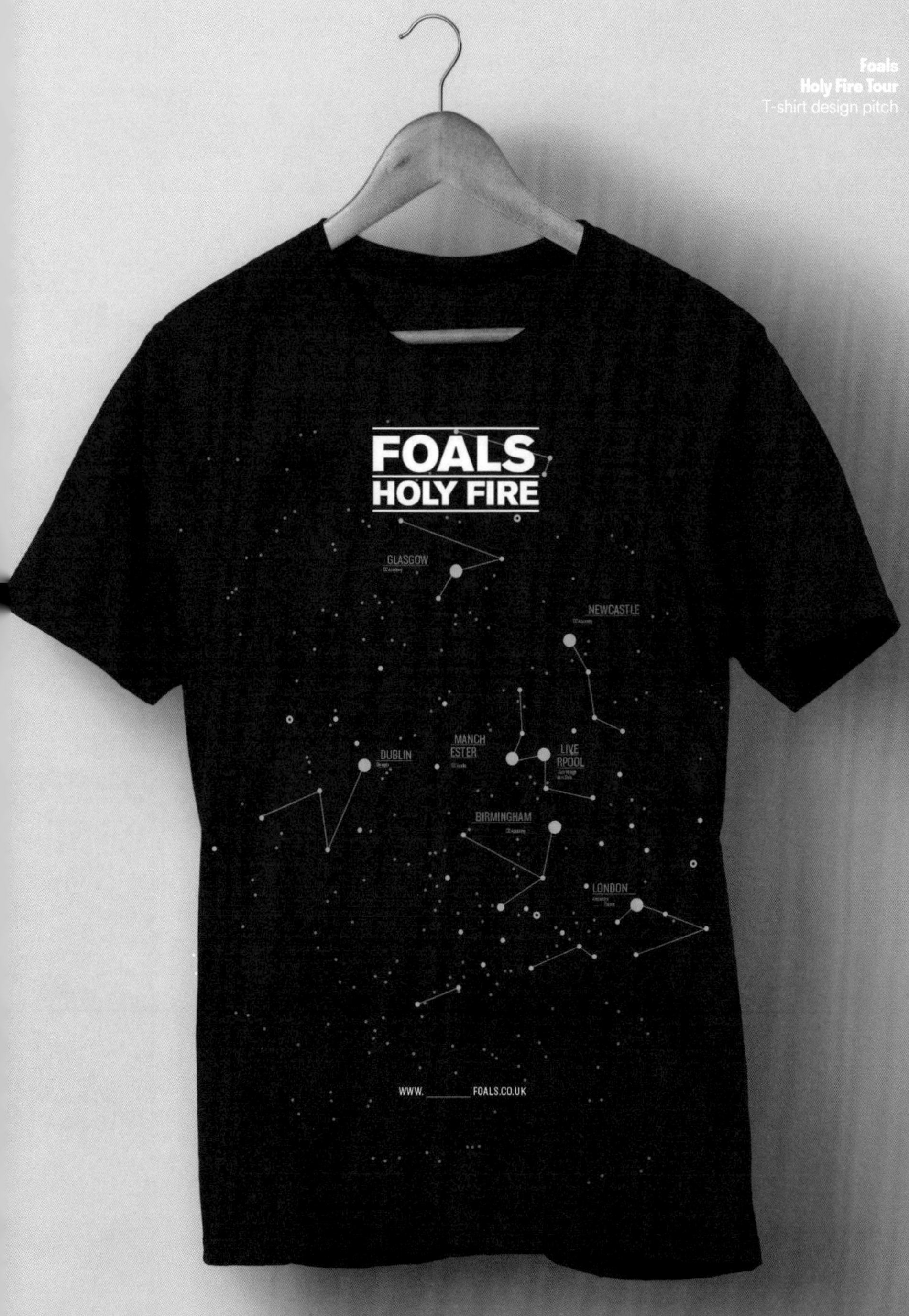

Ciclo Retro
Covent Garden, London
branding + apparel
design concepts

CICLO RETRO VINTAGE BIKES CLOTHING

34 TAVISTOCK STREET, COVENT GARDEN, LONDON

CicloRetro

34
Retro
superior quality

OVER DELIVER DON'T OVERCHARGE

What's the last great customer experience you can remember, where someone went above and beyond to make sure you walked out of their establishment happy? A coffee house can serve the best coffee in town, but bad customer service can make the very same place empty. Unless you like your coffee with attitude, you won't go back.

The need to go that extra mile has never been more important. Long gone are the days of arrogant and stubborn creative directors who would fire any client that would disagree with what they deemed a work of genius. So much so that some agencies today have gone the other way: as long as the client keeps the lights on and staff paid, then anything goes.

The golden equation of budget versus deliverables will always be a dark art of the creative industry. How much is enough and how much is not enough to enable you to deliver someone's dream project?

Smaller projects are the perfect example where every 'extra' counts. We don't want clients to take their new logo and make a pig's ear of its application. Most designers are control freaks, and we don't want somebody else to mess up our meticulously crafted work. Making sure we provide the right solutions - budget permitting or not - should be a priority. Especially if it's something that might take just five minutes of your time.

Going the extra mile should be embedded in our DNA. Delivering an extra few thoughtful items on top of the agreed scope will always provide for a long-lasting impression. It's an approach that turns a one-off customer into a long-term client.

LONDON FILM MUSEUM presents
LIGHTS! CAMERA!
LONDON!

EXHIBITION OPENS
DECEMBER 20

"When a man is tired of London,
he is tired of life for there is
in London, all that
life can afford"
Samuel Johnson 1777

Lights, Camera, London is a new
exhibition presenting how London
has been the setting - and
often the star - of films for
over a century

LONDON
FILM MUSEUM
Covent Garden

45 Wellington Street
London
WC2E 7BN

020 3617 3010
info@londonfilmmuseum.com

londonfilmmuseum.com

Bond In Motion
London Film Museum
branding + design guide + website

londonfilmmuseum.com

London Film Museum & EON Productions present

AN EXCITING NEW FAMILY EXHIBITION

LONDON FILM MUSEUM

BOND IN MOTION

THE LARGEST OFFICIAL COLLECTION OF ORIGINAL JAMES BOND VEHICLES

007

Bond in Motion has over 100 individual original items on display from all 23 James Bond Films. The largest display of its kind ever staged in London.

LONDON FILM MUSEUM
Covent Garden

The exhibition includes concept drawings, storyboards, scripts, model miniatures and full size vehicles from cars, boats, bikes and gyrocopters.

'DOUBLE O HEAVEN'
Time Out

'LICENCE TO THRILL'
Metro

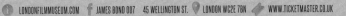

LONDONFILMMUSEUM.COM   JAMES BOND 007   45 WELLINGTON ST.   LONDON WC2E 7BN   WWW.TICKETMASTER.CO.UK   *ticketmaster*

Bond In Motion
London Film Museum
logo design

RULES OF EFFICIENCY

Many creative people see themselves as jugglers or plate spinners every day, and fantasise about being able to handle tons of different tasks. But the more they take on, the more they struggle to focus on the task in hand.

Running a business of any size is a complex task. No company will ever feel they have enough staff to take care of everything: we are fuelled by ambition and technological possibilities that make us strive to do more and more each day.

In a creative business, naturally, a huge chunk of time is spent on creating interesting, engaging and innovative work. At least that's the plan until you find yourself being distracted by email notifications, text messages, phone calls and other elements that should be aiding productivity but do just the opposite. They can be infuriating if we don't use them right.

Personally, I have a love/hate relationship with my inbox. There are days when I think email is an evil entity that just wants me to send more emails. I aim to keep the mail application switched off as much as I can, otherwise, I might as well have chosen a career where I get paid for just answering emails.

Think before you send another email. Try to find another way around it. Pick up the phone and discuss the project in detail, it will save you a very long email chain. After all, you've got more meaningful work to do and it needs your full focus.

PS: Put your all other message notifications on silent mode too or they will keep distracting you all day long. Surely, your tweet reply can wait a minute.

Harry Potter Platform 9 3/4
Kings Cross, London
art direction + ecommerce
—
harrypotterplatform934.com

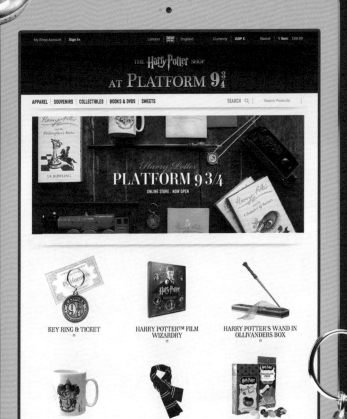

Off the Wall / Opera Browser
website design + development

offthewall.opera.com

 Opera browser

Meet the people   See the experience   Discover the area   Experience Opera

OFF THE WALL
DISCOVER THE AREA

Kjerag is a mountain range, located in Lysefjorden in Forsand municipality, Ryfylke, Rogaland. Its highest point is 1110 m (3642 ft) above sea level. The drop is 984 m (3228 ft) and it is also the site of Kjeragbolten, a 5 m³ stone wedged between two rocks.

BASE jumpers from all over the world come here to fly off its steep mountain sides. The area is a popular climbing destination, with many difficult routes going up its steep faces.

OFF THE WALL
EXPERIENCE OPERA

Crafted in Scandinavia, Opera keeps you online in all kinds of conditions. It's a lightweight, fast app for your phone and computer with Off-Road technology that keeps you online, even in rough conditions.

THE DARK ART OF SIMPLICITY

Some of the most useful, ubiquitous things in our lives
are the ones we don't notice – and the simplest.

How many times have you found yourself using your knife
and fork and celebrating the usefulness of its practical design?
I'm sure it's not been very often. We just accept things,
and we expect stuff to work.

It's the negative or badly designed experiences that we seem
to remember much more. We are far more alert to situations
that are frustrating due to lack of research or good design.

In music, there's a term - the three chord wonder - a music
structure so simple, it is almost always destined for the top
of the charts. Its secret lies in its sheer simplicity.

Through the creative process, we can add extra layers to
our work without adding extra purpose. It can be to satisfy
the client's expectations, because of bad planning or through
a lack of understanding. Clients want to see a return on their
investment, they want to see variations, versions, long hours
spent and phone calls made. Sometimes the simplest and
arguably the best idea is there right from the start but it is
swept aside or overlooked.

When the red lights are ignored, the consequences can be
terrible. I've witnessed an international rebrand go so wrong
that the agency had to create a supporting campaign to explain
the logo to the client and their customers. It's usually when
everything fluffy and insignificant gets binned that the good
stuff makes its way to the forefront.

The simplest yet most functional work can be the hardest
to achieve. But when you get it right, it can be the stuff
that dreams are made of.

**Nathalie Gordon
Photography**
website design

nathaliegordon.com

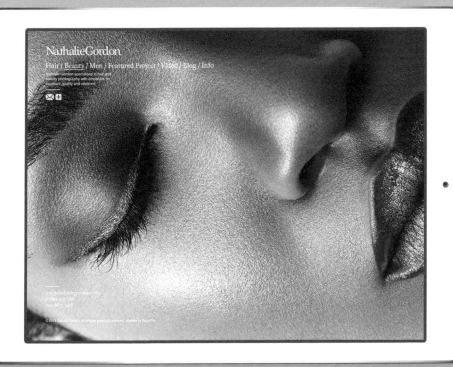

KICKING THE NIGHT SHIFT

When I was building my freelance career I had a full-time job. Every weekday after work, I'd go home, have dinner and do more work. Rarely would I be asleep before 4am. Then, four hours later, I would be getting up for work again. After two years, I quit my day job but continued to work all day and night until the early hours. After five years of late nights, I realised that, although my mind was buzzing, I was running on pure adrenaline and it was taking its toll on my body. It was time to kick the night shift.

I know I've not been alone in this in the creative industry. Sometimes the late nights can seem unavoidable. If there's a mistake or the client moves the goalposts you can then be required to give up your sleep for a night, and different time zones can play a part too. I remember how proud I was to do a 22-hour work day three Mondays in a row due to overlapping work from Sydney, London, and Vancouver, even though I was broken for the other six days of the week. For other night shifts, it's just bad project planning that results in that takeaway pizza order and blurry-eyed work session.

Sleep deprivation affects your brain, memory consolidation, blood pressure and digestive functions, and can result in constant fatigue and disordered moods. Lack of sleep affects your brain in the same way as alcohol – so you might as well go to work drunk. Before your body tells you enough is enough, hopefully, friends or family or partners will have a word with you. Nobody wants to live with a ghost!

The truth is that there's no real need to keep slogging over night shifts. I haven't had to do a late night session in the last five years, but I still produce the same amount of work as I used to. While I'm nowhere near perfect, I'm better organised and more realistic about deadlines and expectations now. When I run out of time in one day, I get up at 5am to make up the time and still hit that 9am deadline. Try to kick the night shift - you will be healthier and happier.

WWF UK
Earth Hour
badge design

WWF UK
Earth Hour
T-shirt design

JOIN THE GLOBAL CELEBRATION

EARTH HOUR

SATURDAY 19 MARCH 2016 | 8.30pm

wwf.org.uk/earthhour | #EarthHourUK

60+

**Exerceo
EMS training**
branding + website

exerceotraining.co.uk

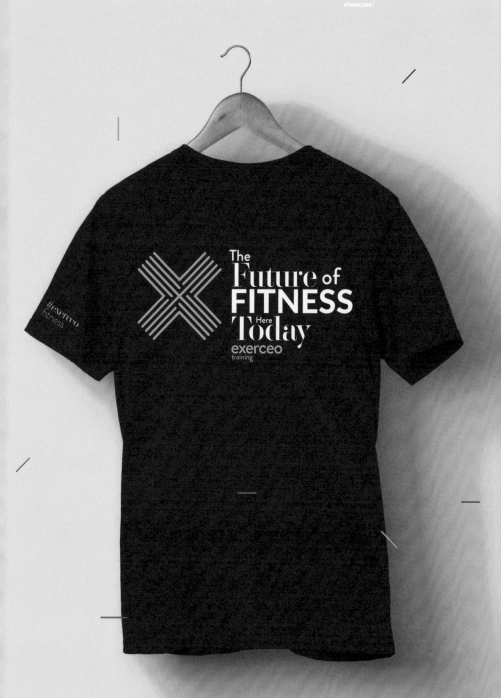

Kate's Originals
World of Muesli
branding
development

KATE'S ORIGINALS

WORLD OF MÜESLI

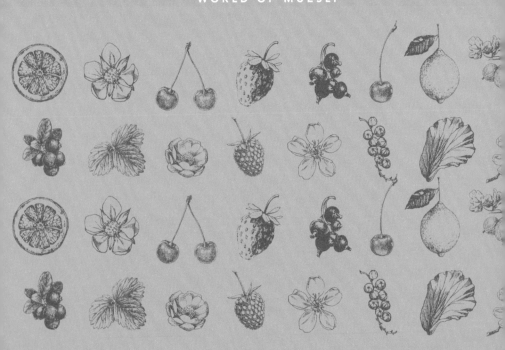

KATE'S
ORIGINALS
WORLD OF MÜESLI

Product
BIRCHER MÜESLI
AN ARTISANAL PRODUCT

WEIGHT   Our Guarantee
1kg   100% ORGANIC   04.14

HANDMADE
IN LONDON

Kate's Originals
stationery
development

KATE'S
ORIGINALS
· WORLD OF MÜESLI ·

Product
CLASSIC MÜESLI
AN ARTISANAL PRODUCT

Weight   Our Guarantee   Use by
1kg   100% ORGANIC   04 14

HANDMADE
IN LONDON

Journei
branding + advertising + website

journei.com

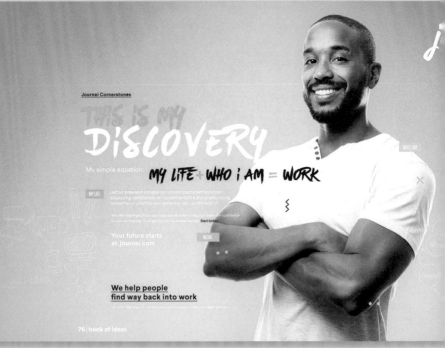

Aaron Phipps
GB wheelchair rugby
branding + website

aaronphipps.com

aaron phipps

Mintlet
pre-paid travel card
branding + website

mintlet.com

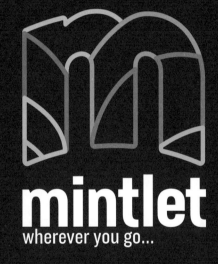

mintlet
wherever you go...

mintlet
wherever you go...

5434 5678 3568 4785

MONTH/YEAR
01/14   **VALID THRU**   **MONTH/YEAR**
01/16

Leon Leondiades

MasterCard

mintlet
wherever you go...

5434 5678 3568 4785

MONTH/YEAR
01/14   **VALID THRU**   **MONTH/YEAR**
01/16

Leon Leondiades

MasterCard

mintlet
wherever you go...

5434 5678 3568 4785

MONTH/YEAR
01/14   **VALID THRU**   **MONTH/YEAR**
01/16

Leon Leondiades

MasterCard

Mintlet
pre-paid travel card
pattern designs

mintlet

COMING SOON
PREPAID TRAVEL CARD AND MOBILE WALLET APPLICATION

Wherever you go... Mintlet's unique interactive and secure multicurrency mobile wallet and card allows you to manage your funds and spend like a local abroad by avoiding those hidden bank charges that are common place when using your domestic debit card or card credit.

Sign up and be notified when Mintlet is ready to launch.

NOTIFY ME

info@mintlet.com   mintlet

**Massive Events Live
South Africa**
branding + website

massiveeventslive.com

Klein
Talent Partners
branding + website

kleintp.co.uk

klein
[talent partners]

Menu ☰

klein talent partners is a London based talent and organisational consulting firm with global reach.

Lectus praesent congue rutrum elit parturient volutpat adipiscing vestibulum vel condimentum a purus adipiscing consectetur ullamcorper senectus vel condimadafdf.

our uniqueness

Lectus praesent congue rutrum elit parturient volutpat adipiscing vestibulum vel condimentum a purus adipiscing consectetur ullamcorper senectus vel condimadafdf.

our work & methods

Lectus praesent congue rutrum elit parturient volutpat adipiscing vestibulum vel condimentum a purus adipiscing consectetur ullamcorper senectus vel condimadafdf.

Lectus praesent congue rutrum elit parturient volutpat adipiscing vestibulum vel condimentum a purus adipiscing consectetur ullamcorper senectus vel condimadafdf.

our impact

klein
[talent partners]

Leadership Team Alignment

The Talent Advantage. Accelerated Executive Talent Solutions. We provide stand-alone and end-to-end, business focused senior talent solutions to impact your overall organisational effectiveness.

Strategic Talent Development

The Organisation Advantage. Holistic Organisation Solutions. We facilitate thorough organisational problem solving processes with your customer's value chain in mind to create sustainable business advantages.

Organisational Effectiveness

The Organisation Advantage. Holistic Organisation Solutions. We facilitate thorough organisational problem solving processes with your customer's value chain in mind to create sustainable business advantages.

Interim Management

The Organisation Advantage. Holistic Organisation Solutions. We facilitate thorough organisational problem solving processes with your customer's value chain in mind to create sustainable business advantages.

about us our people and more

Rest&+Be
guided meditation
branding + design + website

restandbe.com

rest&be

Rest&+Be
laser cut logo

Rest&+Be
set design

photo by
Nathalie Gordon

Krysta Youngs
music artist
logotype

Digital Activation
logo device design

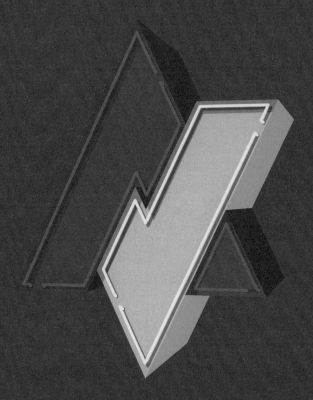

Various logos
design

YOUTH BUSINESS CARIBBEAN

HO

(curlyberry)

CHARLES CARTER HAIR

Est. 1914 BRAND LICENSING Ltd.

W

X-POP

HERA MEDIA

TANYA LACEY

100% DIGITAL

&

NOVEMBER UNIVERSE by Brand Nu™

CicloRetro

Crackpell
associates

ATTENTIVE
by Charlotte Bagg

:you

TILT

in*side*

The Original
FLOWER CELLARS
COFFEE SHOP
COVENT GARDEN

THE
BOSHAM
GALLERY
EST. 2012

NATIONS
LEAGUE

Little BIG
Africa

The Vice Security Group
branding + website

thevicegroup.com

ViceSecurity
Part of the Vice Security Group

ViceSecurity
Part of the Vice Security Group

ViceSecurity
part of The Vice Security Group Ltd

Daniel Karpel
Director

Vice Security | Vice Security Group Ltd.
+ 44 (0) 7540 620 619
dan@thevicegroup.com
thevicegroup.com

YOU
GENERATION

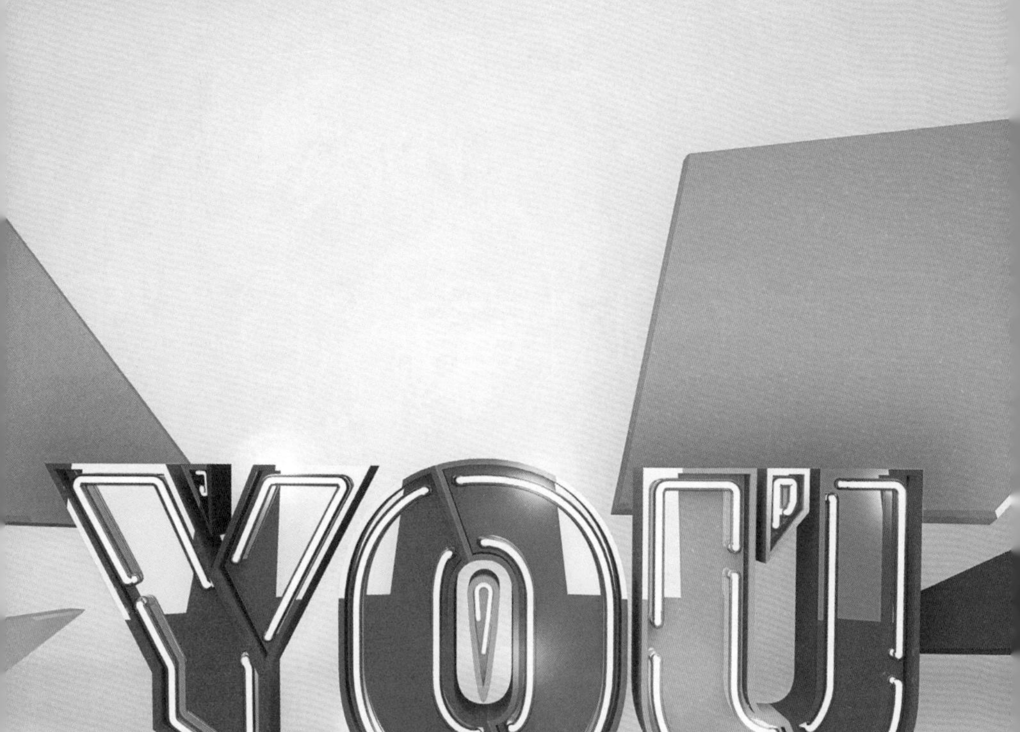
YOU
GENERATION

WGSN London
icon system

technology	camera	shopping basket	spool of thread	sample clothing
badge + lanyard	calendar	pantone chip	swatches	moodboard
pantone chips	browser window	email	document	post-it note
online / action	'you are here'	security	sale	sale
store sign	handbag	shears	price tag	calculator
money	item	poster	note pad	ID

analytics

analytics

analytics

map / plan icon

internet browser

browser - moodboard

post-it note

time - watch icon

coat hanger

fashion / button

browser - live moodboard

ipad

discussion / opinion

spreadsheet

digital

sale

camera

money

analytics

item

returns

video icon

pen

eye icon

store sign

broken box

handbag

factory

supplier

analytics

Explorians
branding + design

explorians.com

explorians
create your own way

We are a community of
explorers, change-makers
and adventuralists - ready
to transform our lives !

Explorians is a personal development incubator designed to help you
find, breed and action new ideas,
projects, career or life changes that
lead you to new possibilities and
help you create your own way.

The Explorer **Purposeful** Living
Relationship Insights **The Expedition**
Exploratory Coaching

explorians.com

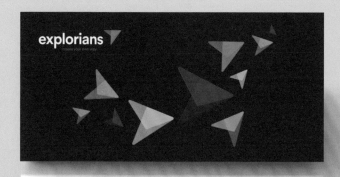

With
_ Compliments

The Explorer Purposeful **Living**
Relationship Vitality The Expedition
Exploratory Coaching

Explorians™ | Klein Talent Partners Ltd.
+ 44 (0) 7946 583014
thorsten.klein@explorians.com
explorians.com

Explorians™ is a trademark wholly owned of Klein Talent Partners Ltd.

Spark Your Life
_ Start The Adventure

31 Linden Gardens
London, W2 4HH
United Kingdom
explorians.com

Explorians™
Klein Talent Partners Ltd.
+ 44 (0) 7946 583014
thorsten.klein@explorians.com

The Explorer Purposeful **Living**
Relationship Vitality The Expedition
Exploratory Coaching

Thorsten Klein
Founder

Explorians™ | Klein Talent Partners Ltd.
+ 44 (0) 7946 583014
thorsten.klein@explorians.com
explorians.com

Explorians
icon system + website

explorians.com

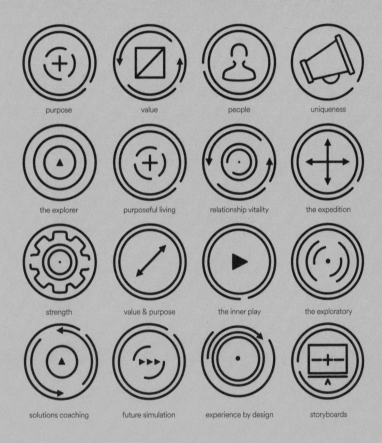

purpose

value

people

uniqueness

the explorer

purposeful living

relationship vitality

the expedition

strength

value & purpose

the inner play

the exploratory

solutions coaching

future simulation

experience by design

storyboards

explorians
create your own way

Programmes   Coaching   Resources   Community   About us   Shop

Spark Your Life.
Start The Adventure.

Do you feel boxed or that your life runs you rather then you making the choices? You have a hunch that there must be another way. We are here to help you reclaim ownership for your life. Create your own way.

Find out more >>

Everything you need to know about us

Welcome to Explorians !

We are a community of seekers, explorers changing matter and adventurers

Vit litis volorempella vollore, voloreped molupta dollam fugitem ni dem inimusci blatis sapid quam re id que quia nem autatiorit faccatur molumqui nit quassitem lam hil ilit apicat. Rehenturem qui occus et voluteni bea dolorematem doloreium qui autemqus aut et et aut faceatem. Everupi deliqui sciati commimi, tet audamus et magnisquam expedis molore, ut quibust a porestem ipid qui .

Are you looking for answers ? Read on ...

Purpose

Values

People

Uniqueness

Social Venture

The Explorians Purpose

We are here to help you create step-changes in your life to become who you truly aspire to be.

Our purpose is to help you create a purposeful life from within and grow beyond your current possibilities. We believe that each one of us holds the inner strengths and resources to become the best version of ourselves. 'As humans, our deepest fear is not to be inadequate, but that we might be powerful beyond measure. Our playing small does not serve anyone.' It is up to each one of us to decide what impact we want to have in our lives and who we want to become. We have created Explorians to help you on this journey and realise inner shifts to leverage your strenghts and potential for your own unique cause. And we do this in a fun, quirky and insightful way through our unique programmes experiences and exploratory coaching.

Got any questions?

Leave us a message. We will get back to you within 2 days.

Name
Enter your full name

Contact telephone
Enter your phone number

Email
Enter email address

Just in case
Confirm your email address

Any comments
Use this space to leave us a message or comment

Send your message

Upcoming Events

Register with us and start your adventure !

25th February 2015
The Explorer

London
Google Campus

Map

Register

Show me: Coaching   Events   Programmes   Webinars   All

Testimonial Your Story

Eped endamus apiet od mod ut volore, sime repellu ptatiis dus, que et ut vero dunt pra di dolupta vide sequisi nciamenducia dolorem porios doluptae.

Vit litis volorempella vollore voloreped molupta dollam fugitem ni dem inimusci blatis sapid quam re id que quia nem autatiorit faccatur molumqui nit quassitem lam hil ilit apicat.

Rehenturem qui occus et voluteni bea dolorematem doloreium qui autemqus aut et et aut faceatem. Everupi deliqui sciati commimi, tet audamus et magnisquam expedis molore, ut quibust a porestem ipid qui ommo quist venis am que nectemque corrore doles sitibusant

Harnham
Data and Analytics
branding + design + website

harnham.com

harnham MARKETING & INSIGHT

harnham INSIGHTFUL RECRUITMENT

SAM JONES
SENIOR MANAGER

1st Floor, Ashville House
131-139 The Broadway
Wimbledon
London SW19 1QJ

T: +44 20 8408 6070
E: samjones@harnham.com
W: **www.harnham.com**

harnham DATA & TECHNOLOGY

harnham CREDIT RISK

harnham INSIGHTFUL RECRUITMENT

MAXIMILIAN KÄMPFE
RECRUITMENT CONSULTANT

Herriottstraße 1
60528 Frankfurt
Deutschland

T: +49 69 677 33 567
E: maximiliankampfe@harnham.com
W: **www.harnham.com**

harnham DIGITAL

harnham DATA SCIENCE

harnham INSIGHTFUL RECRUITMENT

RHYS HORSFIELD
PRINCIPAL RECRUITMENT CONSULTANT

Herriottstraße 1
60528 Frankfurt
Deutschland

T: +49 69 677 33 567
E: rhyshorsfield@harnham.com
W: **www.harnham.com**

Digital
3D icon design

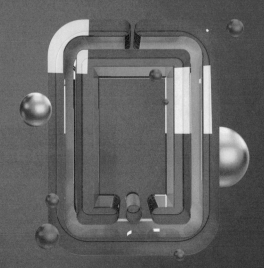

Data Science
3D icon design

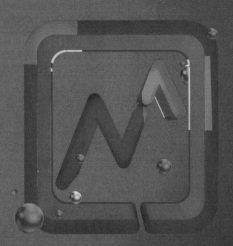

Marketing & Insight
3D icon design

Data & Technology
3D icon design

Harnham
icon system

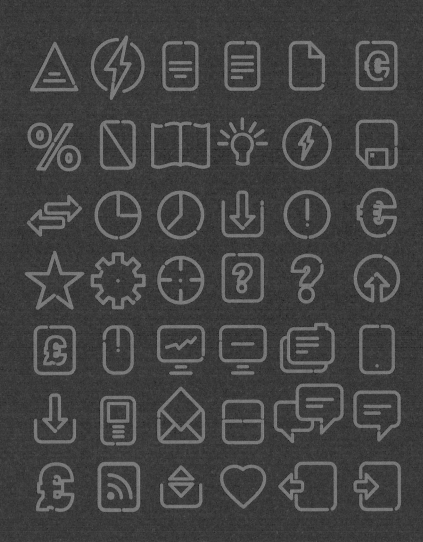

MediaMath
Open EcoSystem
art direction + 3D design

work

New
Marketing
Institute

Helix

T1

MM

Goldman Sachs Foundation
10 000 Businesses
infographic

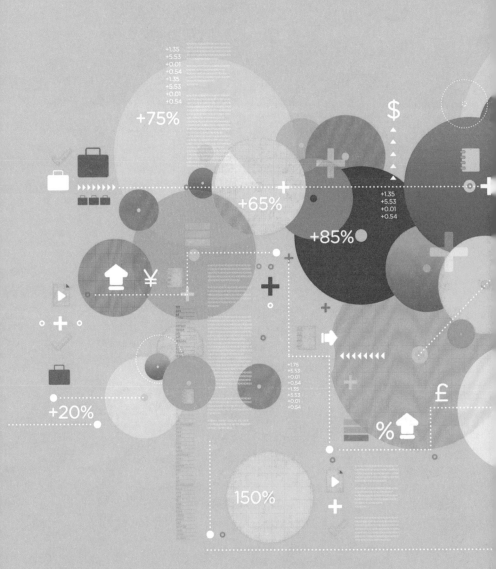

FIGHTING EXCUSES

I am yet to meet a person who would tell me that their career, however illustrious, has been totally free from struggles or regrets.

Everyone has hopes and dreams but not everyone acts on them. We are much better at making excuses than making things happen.

Why do we feel we have to finish up one thing before we can start another? Alternatively, why do we start twenty personal projects and never finish a single one of them? How many sketchbooks do you have that are filled with ideas for projects that are yet to get started?

After trying many ways to conquer this, I've come up with my own solution. I split my year into two halves. For the first six months from January, I embark on the planning stages and sketching of ideas. I simply note down whatever comes to mind and try not to pay too much attention to it. During this time, I tend to think about what I can do with some of these concepts, even if it's just to validate their viability.

For the second six months of the year, I get into design and production. Even when my regular workload is challenging, I weave in personal projects - they are now written on my to-do list every Monday so I can't avoid them. I treat my own projects in the same way I treat client work. And as clients chase on deadline day, I set my own deadlines to ensure my personal work gets done.

I could easily try to spread these personal projects over the course of the whole year, but a having limited time frame works just perfectly for me. Even though I can pick up a project when I feel like working on it, it's the end-of-year urgency that gets the work done. I'm realistic about what I can achieve and I have cut down on making excuses to myself. In fact, I am working on cutting excuses out of my life for good.

COMMIT YOURSELF...
THEN YOU SEE

When I was seven, I joined the local ice hockey team even
though I had never skated on ice before. As a teenager, I formed
a band, but I had never played an instrument before. Soon after
I went on to become a DJ, even though - you guessed it -
I had never stepped in a DJ booth before. From the moment of
deciding to give something a try, I gradually became what I had
set out to become. When I saw an advert for a junior designer
position, I didn't know it was going to be the starting point
for a journey.

As a child, there's no such thing as a long-term plan or worrying
about whether you are going to be any good. You just dive
headfirst into the unknown and you stay there until you work
it out. Fearlessness wins every time.

So why as adults do we feel we need to spend so much extra
time learning something new before we have a go? Why do we
chicken out before we even discover what could be great for us?
Who cares if you're rubbish at something for now: if somebody
else can do it, why can't you?

Everything starts with a spark of imagination, and then you
just need to commit the time and space to dig down into the
inner workings of the subject.

Nobody in life starts at the top but, before you know it, you
could be getting paid for what once was just an idea. Now it's
a fully-fledged career.

We should keep following our instincts and having a go at the
things that make us excited, intrigued and fearless. You never
know how soon you could turn curiosity into a passion, or even
a whole new career.

'Conclusion series'
for NuVango
digital illustration

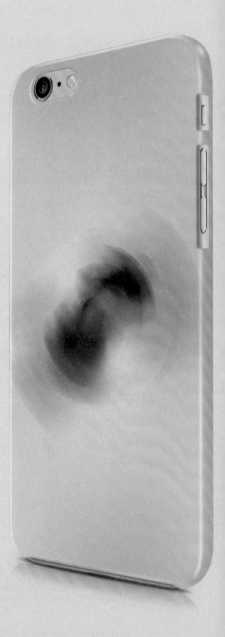

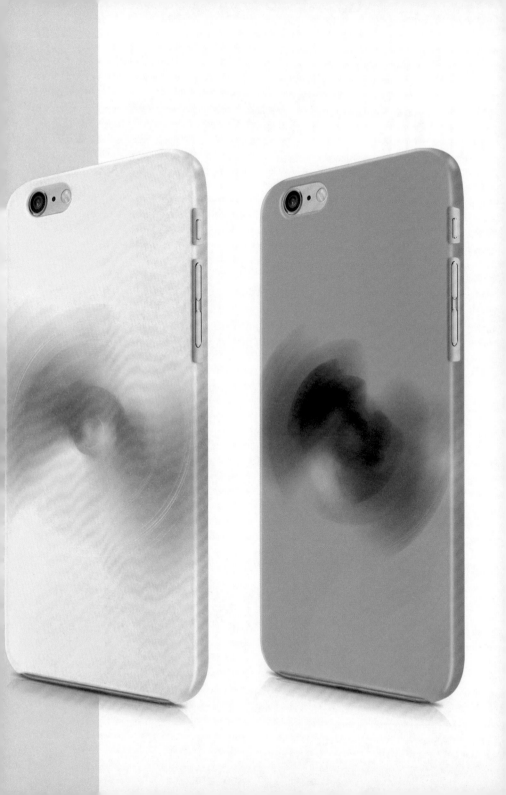

BLACK BELT NINJA SKILLS

In November 2012, Swedish footballer Zlatan Ibrahimovic scored his fourth goal in a friendly match against England. It wasn't just an ordinary set piece, it was an overhead strike where he kicked the ball eight feet high and 40m from the goal. It was awarded Fifa's Goal of the Year and remains one of the best in the history of the game. However, to Zlatan, it was just another of his many incredible goals.

So what is Zlatan's secret? He's not only one of the best footballers in the world, he is also a black belt taekwondo champion. These extra skills have shaped his talent and made him a living legend.

When you're a freelancer answering a broad range of client requests, you can't progress in your career without having extra black belts to your name. All creative disciplines blend into one another: art direction, illustration, graphic design, digital art, retouching, lettering, typography, copywriting, web design and basic coding are just some of the interconnected skills that when brought together bring much better work.

There's never been a better time to learn a new skill. What is it that you have always found fascinating and wondered how to do it? What extra muscle would make your current project go even further? The internet is bursting with websites offering online tutorials and in-depth courses. Collaborate with people who are good at what you're not, and learn that way too.

While taekwondo might not seem to have much in common with football, extra skills provide for added extra magic. Let another world influence you and take you to a place you didn't expect to reach.

HELL IS
EMPTY
AND
ALL THE
DEVILS
ARE HERE

WILLIAM SHAKESPEARE

'We'
personal project

WE KNOW WHAT

WHAT WE

WILLIAM

WE ARE, BUT NOT

MAY BE

SHAKESPEARE

666 Denim
Collaboration project
digital illustration

The
KNOWN

& the
# UNKNOWN

SAMURAI KNOWLEDGE

It's exciting to know that I can learn something new today that will make me think differently about tomorrow. Learning is free and it can be truly addictive. But the more I know, the more I realise how little I know.

This is how I approach my work. When you spend years learning the foundations of your craft, you have to spend even longer understanding everything else around you.

Design isn't just for designers - it rules everything. Everything should be designed with people in mind. Neuroscience, biometrics, big data, performance analytics - these extra tools are used by brands to make customers come back time and time again. We are being constantly observed online with algorithms ticking away in the background recording our every move.

As a graphic designer, you might wonder what neuroscience has to do with designing a brochure or poster. But having a little understanding of science, marketing strategies, customer relations or selling techniques will give you the edge over your peers.

The more we understand ourselves, the better the work we create. When you show an understanding of what you do and why, your clients will buy into you before they buy into your work. This is your samurai knowledge that goes beyond your job title.

When I was in my late teens, I wanted to be a rock star and not bother with higher education. I'm glad things turned out otherwise. I went on to study economics, which helped me immensely in my design career. Now, many years later, I would happily go back to full-time education. I want to keep on learning.

Us
by David Nicholls
rejected book
cover design

**Great Online Shopping Festival
w/ Google Labs Singapore**
digital illustration + retouch

**Great Online Shopping Festival
w/ Google Labs Singapore**
digital illustration + retouch

DO MORE AND DO IT BETTER

"Do one thing and do it well": I'm sure you're very familiar with this saying. As creatives, we can often be encouraged to specialise in one style or discipline, but I believe in more.

Imagine a recording studio. In one corner there's a session guitarist, at the mixing desk is the producer. The session guitarist is the best in town. But the producer can play the guitar too. If our guitar hero didn't turn up today, the producer could easily have recorded that part and nobody would know the difference. The same could have also applied for drums, keys or bass. That's how the producer got to where he is, overseeing recording sessions to get the best out of everyone.

The guitarist is a specialist, and so is the producer. Both do one thing extremely well, but there's a huge difference in their skill set. I don't see the producer as a generalist – to me, he's a multi-skilled specialist. Our guitarist delivers the best guitar solos, the producer delivers the best albums.

Specialists in the creative industries can be illustrators, letterers, copywriters or 3D designers - these guys are happy with just one label. They are your session musicians. Call them any time to help with the gig. They will add some magic.

If you are a designer, director or producer, you can't deliver just one type of work over and over. Your career wouldn't last more than a year. Constant repetition is a killer.

Your point of difference lies in how much you're willing to put yourself out there to deliver an outstanding project. The key is taking your specialism and adding expertise as you go along. No producer was ready as a teenager. They listened, learned and understood. Learn to play the solos, and then you can deliver the albums.

showcase

THE 100 SONGS RULE

The smell, taste or the look of something new - whether it's music, fashion or design style - can be very tempting. However, sometimes these influences can prove to be disruptive. How do you discover what type of work you want to focus on? You need to start somewhere.

In music, there's a piece of advice for new bedroom producers: make 100 songs in as many styles, then you'll know what you truly like and what you're good at. Find yourself in one of these styles.

In my early twenties, I got my first proper graphic design job in a fairly small design and print company, where I stayed for two and a half years. When I started, I was instantly thrown in at the deep end. I went to work on pretty much everything from flyers and brochures to gig posters, logos, stationery design and much more. This was just work for regular clients with regular expectations. At the beginning, I was wide-eyed and had the opportunity to learn on the job. I made a ton of mistakes that I quickly learned from.

Gradually, I started to mould the shape of my personal style. I stopped just getting the work done and began to enjoy my work even more. It took me roughly 800 pieces of work to realise what I liked, what I disliked, what I was good at and where I wanted to go next. This was my design incubation period. When I look back, it was the best possible way to find my true voice.

This was my equivalent of 100 songs. I kept playing, breaking and exploring, and eventually found the inner voice that helped me quit my job to go freelance.

Try everything at least once. Take your time and keep exploring.

**Carmine Rose
'Naked'**
album artwork
concepts

**Jupitaroise
Desktopography**
digital illustration

RUNNING AWAY FROM THE HERD

Beginning a new career can throw you back to when you started school. You can opt to be that lonely kid whose best friends are books, or you can hang out with the people you'll share your first cigarette with behind the bike shed. In the creative industry, this is a bit like an artist and a bunch of designers: often an artist strives for peaceful creative solitude, whereas designers tend to hunt in packs. Especially online.

People like to surround themselves with familiar things. We don't like change too much. We think we do, but just have a think about the number of similar jumpers in your wardrobe. I bet you there's very clear pattern of repetition.

Starting out in the creative industry can be a daunting task, so we naturally gravitate towards a pack and stick to it. We want to be accepted, cherished and celebrated; so our style is likely to be influenced by elements of others' work, on top of which we might add principles of a fleeting trend. When our work resembles that of established leaders, we tend to think we are in a safe place. The truth is the opposite.

It's time to break out and rejoin the unique path we set out to forge in the first place. It's time to leave the collective mindset behind. Safe never inspires action.

Everybody is unique and that should shine through the work we create. Find your strangeness and stick with it. Don't worry about the herd. Make your own world.

THE ART OF DESIRE PATHS

To navigate problems, we invent shortcuts, hacks, and improvised solutions — even if we're not aware of doing so.

Every city, town or village has at least one narrow footpath in the middle of a public green space. Town planners design pavements but we often ignore them and take the shortest route. I always aim to make my own paths instead of taking the pre-set roads.

When you step aside and observe the actions of others, you quickly realise there's always another way to solve a problem. You can learn through observation and find your own way. Just because somebody tells you to do something in a certain way, it doesn't mean it's the correct way. You can always give it a try, but it should never stop you from looking further.

How many times do you click something in the top left corner of your screen when a keyboard shortcut could have done the same task more quickly? How often do you travel to work without trying another route which could actually be quicker or more enjoyable? When you take a step away and look at your life and work, you will find dozens and dozens of actions that could be made much quicker or simpler.

We have hard-wired natural instincts but our own set of navigational controls. This is why we have focus groups, eye detection software, neuroscience and lots of other scientific gadgetry to help us understand how much we are alike or different. Our uniqueness creates variety in the world.

Create desire paths, keep looking, keep solving.

Dolby Atmos
w/ Hatch SF
digital illustration

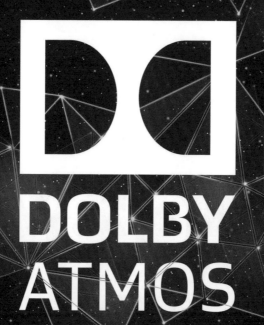

**Dolby Atmos Home
w/ Hatch SF**
digital illustration

**Dolby Atmos Cinema
w/ Hatch SF**
digital illustration

Dolby Atmos Mobile
w/ Hatch SF
digital illustration

**Dolby Atmos Rave
w/ Hatch SF**
digital illustration

#unmasked
OFFF Barcelona 2015
B is for Brave
typography

Character no.26
custom alphabet design

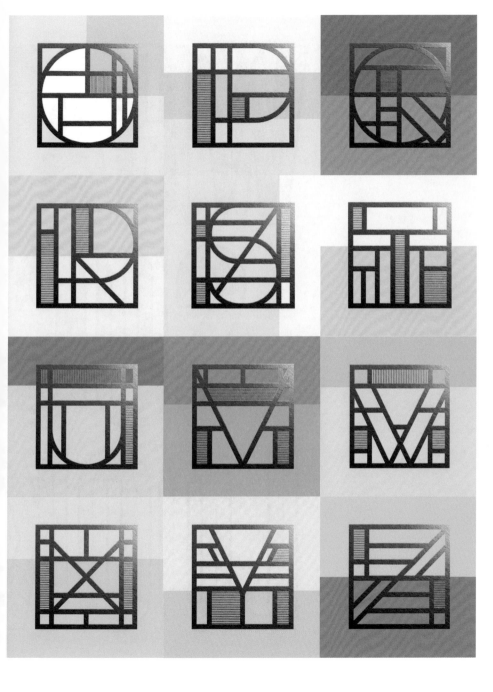

Agency Core
Success series
typographic poster

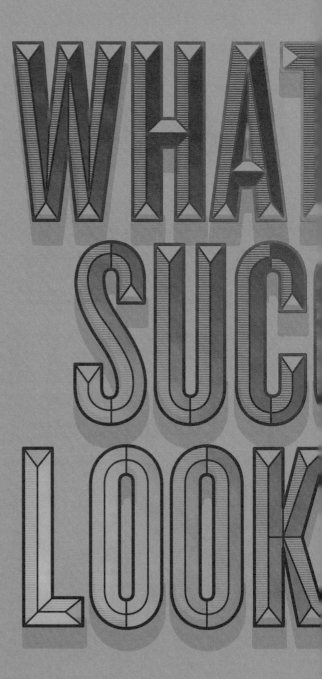

DOES ESS LIKE?

Raleigh Ritchie
Spring Tour
merchandise design

THE WORLD IS AT
MY FEET AND I AM
STANDING ON THE
CEILING, AND I FALL,
FALL, FALL WHEN IT ALL
COMES DOWN, AND I
WON'T BE CRUSHED BY
THE WEIGHT OF THIS
TOWN, I FALL FROM THE
SKY BUT I WON'T FALL
FOREVER, I FALL, BUT
WHEN I RISE I'LL BE
STRONGER THAN EVER

MIRACLES CAN HAPPEN ON ANY SIZE WAVE

Creativity isn't meant to be easy. If it was, we would lose interest pretty quickly. When you take a surfboard out into the ocean, you have to wait for the right moment before you get to ride a wave. Even then, a wave is hardly ever perfect. But when you fall off your board, you pick yourself up and rush back into the sea. When it all clicks, it gives you a sense of achievement. The creative process is just like that. Seeing a project through from start to finish will give you that warm fuzzy feeling of wanting to go and start something new again. It's addictive.

To be a good surfer or a good designer takes long hours of practice. But when you start seeing results, all the bruises become badges of honour.

When I first started working in graphic design, it all seemed fun – until clients came along. I felt I was in daily battles and I didn't seem to be winning many of them. It took hundreds of projects before I worked out the best way of handling clients and their expectations, demands, and limitations. I gradually worked out a way to understand, process and enjoy this type of work. Ten years later I believe that graphic design isn't fun until the client comes through the door. We need them to make great things happen.

We need to dispel the common myth that only good designers can have good clients. Through ambitious work, you can put your clients into that category. It doesn't matter if your clients are big brands or companies that no one has yet heard of, you can be an integral part of their success.

So, take your surfboard and paddle out to sea. It doesn't matter what type of waves you're riding today, just aim for the best ride. You will soon find out that miracles can happen on any sized wave.

'Miracles'
for November Universe
apparel design

CREATIVITY AS A TOOL TO HELP OTHERS

In January 2015, I was standing in the middle of a village in Uganda, a stone's throw from the hills of the Kenyan border. The place was filled with families who had huge smiles on their faces. The air was spinning with particles of red dust while children ran around and played happily. In the corner of the yard, I noticed the colours and shapes of the logo that I designed in my studio back in London. I was there to see the work of Little Big Africa, a charity that brings water sources to remove villages.

Almost exactly a year earlier, I agreed to rebrand the charity and to provide them with the look and feel of an established international organisation. And I wanted to know what else I could do to help.

The success of a branding project can be measured in many different ways. Sometimes it's extra revenue or an increase in market share. As a result of LBA's rebrand, it attracted more volunteers than ever before. Success meant extra help on the ground, and subsequently a life-changing impact on the people I met in the village.

I didn't know I could make a real difference until I worked on my first charity project many years ago. Since then, I have discovered that it is possible to assist many worthy causes and be part of amazing movements.

So if you work with the boys in suits, think about how you can help those who need help but can't afford it. Anyone with a talent of any kind can make a difference. Next time you see an advert for a charity, think about how you could help. You have the skills and knowledge to give something very important.

You could create something portfolio-worthy and help an organisation save time, funds and maybe even lives. Money can't buy such feeling.

LITTLE
INTERVENTIONS
BIG
IMPACTS

BIG
Africa

LITLEBIGAFRICA.ORG

OPEN YOUR EYES

Inspiration is a cocktail of experiences, moments, scents, sounds and feelings that leave a lasting impression and an irresistible urge for action. Keep your eyes and ears open wherever you go, whatever you do. When you pay attention to the world around you, it will give you reasons to create work that others will take notice of.

People like to stick with like-minded souls and they don't always like their views challenged. But why would you spend all your life eating only one type of cuisine? Why would you listen to just one genre of music?

We need more cross-pollination and to break out of our groups. For example, illustrators hardly ever hang out with typographers and don't even get me started on the electric fenced world of web developers and user experience folks. Why don't we share more with one another? Why don't we have a conversation with people from all walks of life and really listen to how they go about their profession?

We need to start looking at the other worlds around us. Doing that forces you to stop, think and question. When you question everything around you, you get plenty of fresh answers that you can implement in your work.

It's a magical moment when a hit of inspiration strikes and you manage to make a speck of an idea into something huge. But inspiration, like happiness, can't often be found if you look for it. It will find you when you least expect it.

For now, keep talking to people, taking pictures, making voice memos, writing notes, keeping a scrapbook or just tearing out pages of magazines. It's all about building a library of these small yet significant moments. When you keep them all in one place, every time you go back there you'll find something new.

LA Magazine
vector illustrations

THE RULE OF THE OPPOSITE

An average design is a means to an end, good work gets the job done, but great work gets people talking. Great work doesn't rely on clichés; it stimulates thoughts, actions and movement. It's great because it was made with substance and ambition. It surprises people, and it makes them envious for not having that idea first. Great work is rare. Good work can be found. Average work is everywhere.

One way to decipher the enigma of great creative work is the rule of the opposite. Discard the obvious choices and dig deeper to find something which answers the brief in a much more exciting way. Work harder to find the genius.

Here's a simple exercise - let's put together a logo brief for a company that sells organic food. You can set up your brand values and target demographic. Let's name the company 'Fresh'. What are your initial thoughts on the logo design? Simple type, maybe a minimal font and logo device - maybe a little green leaf? What other ideas come flooding to you? Take a mental note of a few options. Next, open a web browser and do a Google image search for the name of this company. It's more than likely that your initial idea is waiting for you there. It's been done zillion times before because a zillion 'designers' thought it would be a good way of solving the brief.

People like to engage with what you create and will reward you for making them stop and think for a while. There's no need to take the obvious route just because you can get your job done in five minutes. Creating engaging work should be an everyday task. Kick out the clichés for good.

Birger Jarl
10ar anniversary
vector type
illustration

birgerjarl

'Sun'
type
experiment

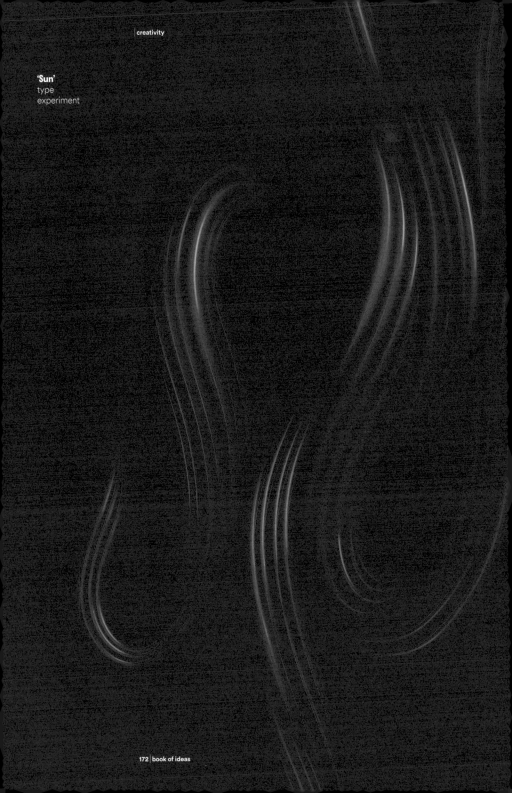

'You are'
digital
typography

You are
sweet
as
Sugar

TURNING DUST INTO GOLD

Most creative people combine their work with operating their own personal media company. Each of us has at least one channel of 'curated content,' created from the little smart device in our pocket. But do we pay much attention to other people's channels or even our own digital footprints?

Each day tens of millions images are uploaded everywhere online. Ideas are viewed around the world: some images are liked, some are forgotten - even by the person who posted them. Yet we can become addicted to the numbers and interactions, and this cycle can make us miss a moment of creative genius.

Fantastic work is everywhere, not just online. When you do a little inventory of your computer hard drive, there are bound to be pieces of work with the potential to be amazing. It doesn't matter how old the work or sketch is: a good idea doesn't have an expiry date and there's no excuse to let it die.

How about turning that idea into a physical object? It doesn't matter if you are making apparel, wallpapers, badges, sculptures or printing posters – you will reform a connection with what your creativity stands for. Digital files will never have that smell of fresh ink. You could be amazed at the reactions when you share or even sell your work.

It doesn't have to cost the earth to make these things happen. You become your own client, which can be both testing and rewarding. You'll make mistakes and you'll learn. It's a risk worth taking.

Take an idea, turn it upside down and see what you can discover. You can never predict where it will take you, but along the way, you might turn dust into gold.

'Numbers'
w/ Creo Design
full sculpture line up

'Autumn Sunset'
original drawing

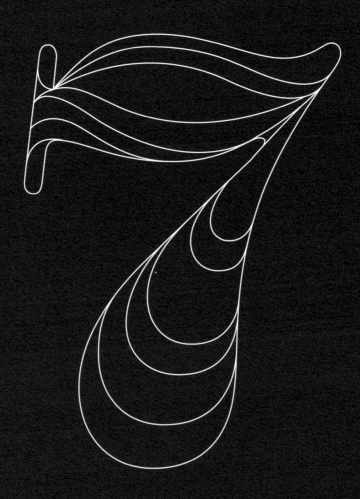

Proctor & Gamble
London 2012 exhibition
2x8m hand-written typography project

WHERE IDEAS COME TO LIFE

Creative minds enjoy an abundance of thoughts and ideas every day, even if sometimes it feels like the opposite.

If you commute to work, you'll likely spend that time worrying about a late train rather than focusing your brain on solving an impossible project conundrum. You might be saving yourself for the 'ideas-on-demand' brainstorming session at work. But ideas can't always be produced immediately – something good can take time to shape itself from a rough diamond into a gem.

There's a ton of noise occupying our minds, lives and office spaces and it can be really hard to tune into the right channel. Even as I write this sentence I keep being distracted by thoughts of tomorrow's deadlines. It can be hard to keep focus in the daily whirlwind.

So much good thinking happens while we do essential tasks that don't require much mindful presence. When I look back at my past projects, I can pinpoint the moments where each idea came to me. It hardly ever happened on the computer. Ideas come when I am standing in the crowd at a concert, wandering through a gallery, making my way down a busy high street, playing guitar, in an airport lounge or walking my dog.

They arrive when you feel the least worried about things like deadlines or paperwork or admin. It's only when you stop thinking so much that you start to hear yourself and shape ideas.

'Original ColourSpaces'
Computer Arts Magazine
digital typography

The ORIGINAL COLOUR SPACES ESTABLISHED 1810

Cadbury Australia
typographic
ad campaign

FORGET TEXTING YOUR MUM XOX.

GO GIVE HER A REAL XOX.

BUY A BLOCK   ENTER ONLINE   SEND A BLOCK   SHARE A BLOCK

BEEN A WHILE? WIN A BLOCK TO SHARE WITH SOMEONE SPECIAL. SEE SPECIALLY MARKED PACKS OR CADBURY.COM.AU

YOUR NANNA DOESN'T DO WEBCAM. IF YOU WANT TO SEE HER GO SEE HER

BUY A BLOCK   ENTER ONLINE   SEND A BLOCK   SHARE A BLOCK

BEEN A WHILE? WIN A BLOCK TO SHARE WITH SOMEONE SPECIAL. SEE SPECIALLY MARKED PACKS OR CADBURY.COM.AU

SETTING EXTRA CHALLENGES

Imagine you have the opportunity of a solo show of your work in a gallery. The space is in central London and you can do whatever you like. The sky's the limit and all that.

Are you interested? Excited? Scared? Does it feel right? Well, of course, you'd say a big fat yes!

Now for the small print: you've got one month to come up with the show before it opens. Still interested?

This was the exact opportunity given to me a few years ago when I was offered a gallery space for a month. I never have or never will think of myself as an 'artist,' but there I was.

In true designer style, I started to create a problem so I could look for solutions. The gallery was in London's West End, so I looked to the area's theatrical heritage for inspiration. I invented a graphic design musical about the West End's bright lights and magical characters to celebrate that weird and wonderful world paved with so many inspiring stories. I zig-zagged the streets of London looking for visual clues, pored over books and scoured the internet.

I could have made it easy for myself and just put up a stylistic repeat of something I knew well. Everyone has a house style. Instead, I went for a crazy typographic experiment - I wanted to challenge myself to justify the weight of the experience. I didn't want to make it easy for myself.

The gallery show featured a set of ten futuristic, neon-like typographical illustrations and I wrote a short poem to accompany each piece. It was all worth the effort to make the project such a special piece in my portfolio.

The West End Show by Brand Nu
The Nancy Victor Gallery, London
solo exhibition

thewestendshow.co.uk

**The West End Show
by Brand Nu**
exhibition poster

thewestendshow.co.uk

HOLBORN

WINGS OF ORANGE MIST

Giddy nights
echo servings of laughter,
concrete crescent with see-through walls
noble guest, so sought-after.

See-through walls looking in,
concrete crescent, so sought-after,
giddy nights
servings sparse with laughter.

COVENT
GARDEN

TWO FOR A POUND

Vivid colours,
narrow rushing streets,
petal coated piercing sounds,
amazement built, imagination struck.

Rushing sounds,
piercing colours,
petal coated streets,
imagination struck, amazement built.

TRAFALGAR SQUARE

A THOUSAND SHADOWS

A feral bunch in riotous assembly
casting shadows on the ground,
nourishment
from a thousand finger tips.

A thousand shadows
cast iron assembly,
culture
from a thousand finger tips.

SEVEN DIAL

BOILING THE PENNIES

One direction
a thousand paths,
a rhyme of footsteps
a story untold.

A rhyme of paths
a history of footsteps
a direction untold.

CHARING
CROSS

CONCRETE QUARTET

A rhythmical beat
counts the number
of London's street
and place of slumber.

A steady drum
reaches the place
of London's street
and unknown face.

SO HO

SHINE A LIGHT

A stream of intoxicating emotions
swells the veins of ambition,
stories penned, stories told,
muffled words.

An intoxicating stream of words
swells the veins of emotion,
stories told, stories lost,
muffled ambition.

Tanya Lacey
Now That You're Gone
single sleeve design

TANYA LACEY
NOW THAT YOU'RE GONE

1. NOW THAT YOU'RE GONE
2. NOW THAT YOU'RE GONE [LADY LESHURR REMIX]
FEAT. LADY LESHURR

Written by: T.Lacey, M.Schwartz, J. Reynolds
Produced/Mixed by: James F Reynolds and Matt Schwartz
Mastered by: Jeremy Cooper for Soundtrap.

www.tanyalaceyofficial.com

©2013 Laceywood Records

FOR PROMO USE ONLY

Laceywood records

TANYA LACEY NOW THAT YOU'RE GONE

Carmine Rose / EP ii
album sleeve design

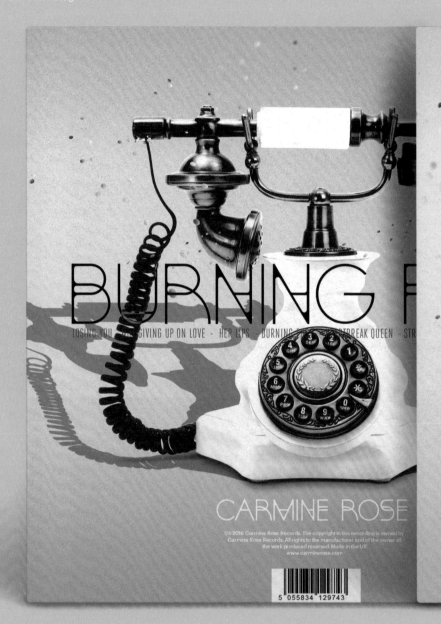

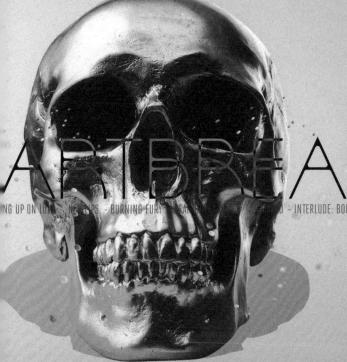

CARMINE ROSE

5 055834 129743

B L R K

M R K S

N O U R

& B R A N D

N U

Nour EP
BLK MRKS + Brand Nu
artwork + 6 track EP + music video

nour-ep.com

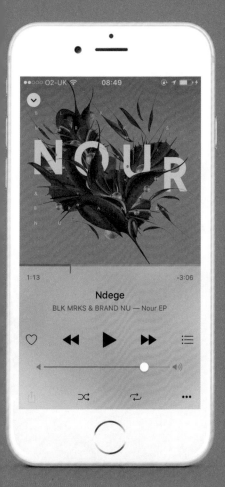

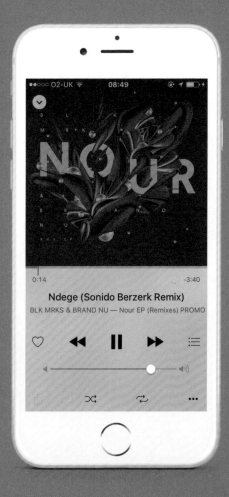

Nour REMIX EP
BLK MRKS + Brand Nu
album artwork

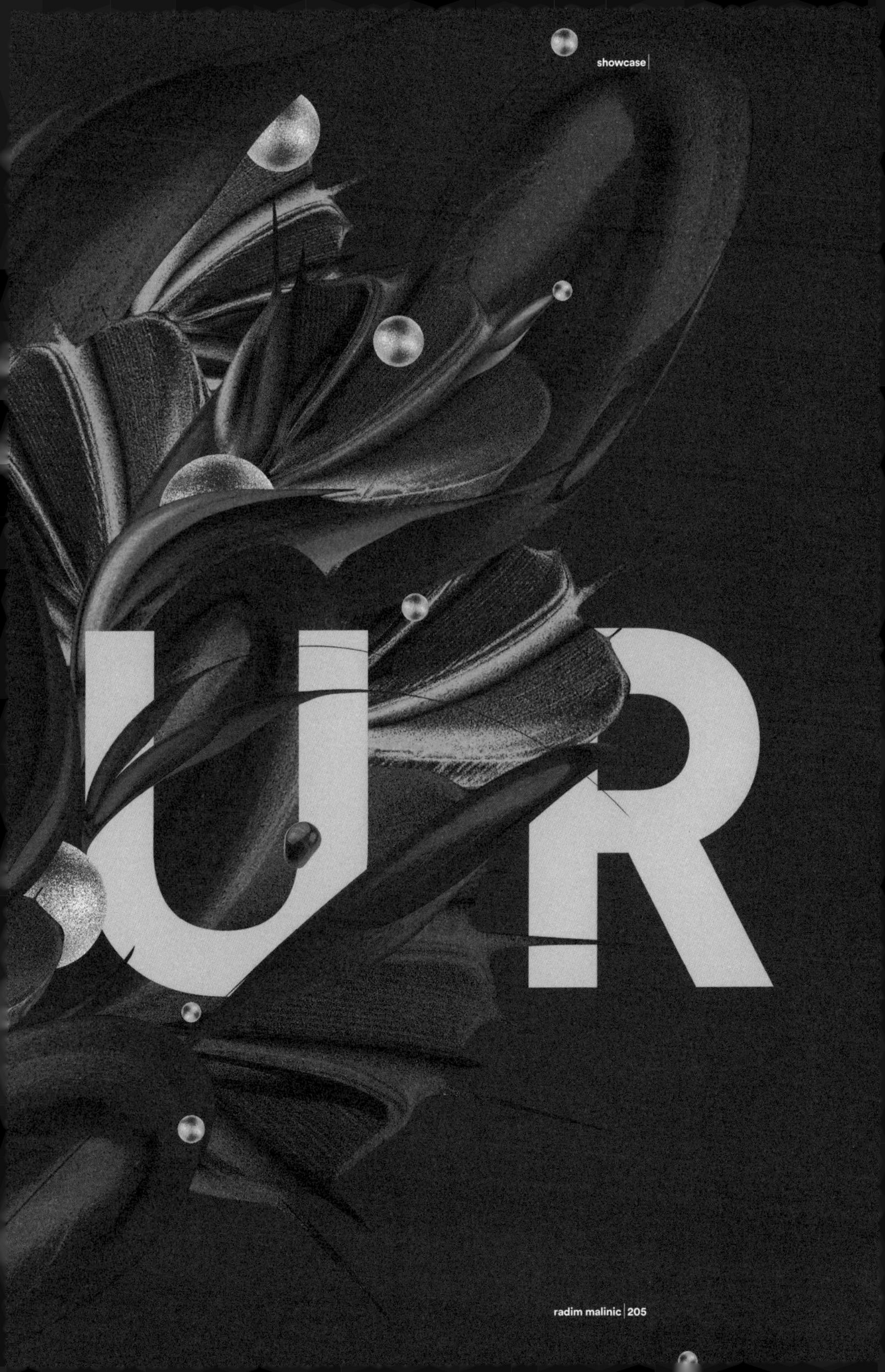
UR

Extra Dry Records
branding

PURVEYORS OF THE FINEST SOUND

EXTRA
DRY

extradry.tv

Various Artists
Balearic Jams EP
retouch + artwork

Extra Dry Records
Mele v Ridney - Got the answer
retouch + artwork

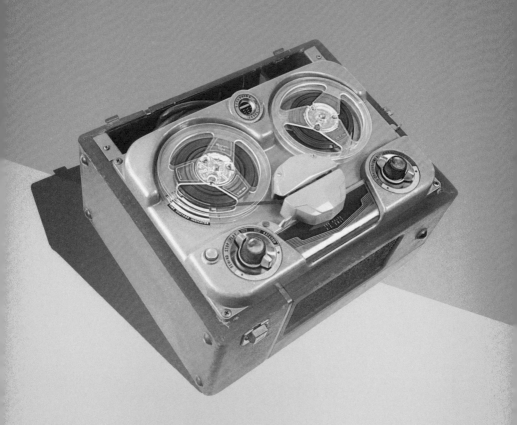

Stephen McCleery
Don't take this pain away
digital illustration + album artwork

A. Soy Mustafa's Rework
B1. Original Mix*
B2. Soy Mustafa's Riot in Acid Mix

Original written and produced by Stephen McCleery
Vocals by Laura Vane
Mastered by Stephen McCleery & Toby Vane
at www.zanzibarproduction.com
Additional production and remix by
Soy Mustafa @ Cinema Verite, London.

Published by Shack Music / Copyright Control
P&C Shack Music 2013

Cat No SM020

info@shackmusic.com
www.shackmusic.com
www.istephenmccleery.com

Stephen McCl
ft. Laura Vane

DON'
THIS
AWAY

DON'T TAKE
THIS PAIN
AWAY

Cinematic Label
Soy Mustafa - Bipolars Revenge
type design + album artwork

Cinematic Label
Reggie Dokes - Child of the Sun EP
type design + album artwork

**Cinematic Label
Visionaries Series**
album sleeve design

CINEMATIC LABEL presents

EDANTICONF
- HIGHWAY OF
THOUGHTS EP

CINMV12006

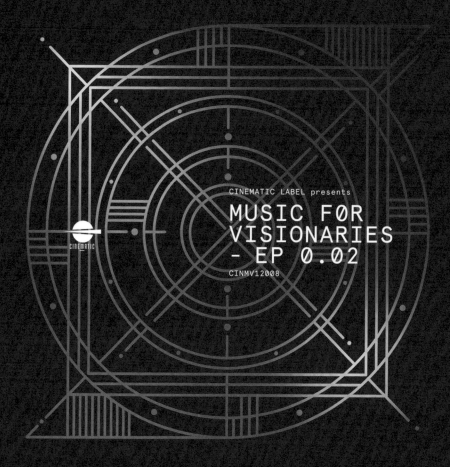

CINEMATIC LABEL presents

MUSIC FØR
VISIONARIES
- EP 0.02

CINMV12008

**Cinematic Label
Visionaries Series**
album sleeve design

CINEMATIC LABEL presents

MUSIC FOR
VISIONARIES
- EP.0.01

CINMV12005

CINEMATIC LABEL presents

FUMIHIRO HOSHI
& TADAC
- AURORA EP

CINMV12007

Cinematic Label
CINMV12002 - 04
album sleeve designs

CINEMATIC LABEL - CINMV12002
FLORIAN MULLER
YOU
EP

CINEMATIC LABEL - CINMV12003
JOHANNES VOLK
DESERT
LABYRINTH
EP

CINEMATIC LABEL - CINMV12004

JEROFOU
FIERE
ALLURE
EP

FACE A FEAR EVERY DAY

Fear should be the fuel for action. We will always face fears, and they can rule our thoughts, deeds and diaries. They can prevent greatness from happening as they cloud our decisions.

The first step to making changes in your life is to expose your fear by admitting it to yourself. There's no better place to fight uncertainty than when you're in a public space: there, you have no way of going back on your decision. For that reason, I chose public speaking as the place to tackle my anxiety.

Any industry conferences are full of designers, developers or thinkers all keen to tell their story on the main stage, but they can spend weeks leading up to their talks fearing some kind of failure on the day.

While some seasoned professionals have battled their fears over and over, many still get that queasy feeling in their stomachs. But there is such a thing as positive stress. Anxiety is best turned into positive energy: it means you care about what is about to happen. You give a shit.

As someone who has experienced these moments of overwhelming anxiety, and not just on the stage, I have purposely put myself forward for as many conferences as possible. I didn't want to just sit tight and wait for the day the fear might go away. The more talks I've done, the better I have structured my presentation and my delivery has improved. When I see others deliver, I know I can do it too.

So many top singers and actors have felt and still feel the same, and it didn't let their fears stand in the way of their careers. We are all made from the same stuff - we are all capable of great achievements.

If they can do it, you can. If not better.

MONTREAL MEETS iii present the exclusive premiere of

MONTREAL MEETS

WHEN.WORLDS.COLLIDE

by Radim Malinic [Brand Nu™] . London . UK

We live in the world where edges are getting increasingly more blurred with addition of new technology. The unknown today becomes the normality of tomorrow. As a result, the world of traditional design is now inevitably changing, colliding with other influences. So, let's take time to find a unified image without confusing the main objective - simplicity of understanding.

THÉÂTRE TELUS - MONTRÉAL 🍁

1280 RUE ST-DENIS / COIN STE-CATHERINE. H2X 3J6

05.28.13 10AM

www.montrealmeets.ca
www.brandnu.co.uk

TAKE A DEEP BREATH

How can you get stressed doing a job you love? Surely it can't be stressful sitting at your desk, listening to music, browsing through font books and choosing the right Pantone colour?

However, when you throw into the mix emails, phone calls, estimates, pitch work, printer quotes, web developer briefings, conference calls, more emails, accounts, tax returns, notifications, broken computers, to-do lists, to-do list apps, blogging, internet connection issues, website updates, social media updates, more emails, Skype calls... oh, and life, things become more complicated.

It's so easy for all these things to hijack our minds and put us on course for burnout. Sometimes it takes our engines grinding to a halt before we realise we can't carry on like this – trapped in stress and anxiety, or even the start of something more serious.

One of the ways to stay on top of things is to control your breathing. When the mind gets tense, it affects the body. Be mindful and observant during a work day and you'll find out how often your breathing is out of control. You might find yourself holding your breath when reading client emails or be in situations with immense pressure where stress takes over. Keep an eye on your mind and breathing. Take a deep breath and pause for a minute.

Setting aside a few minutes several times a day can stop your world from getting crazy. These tiny changes within you can make the outside world a more manageable place.

Take a deep breath, hold it and exhale. Repeat.

DREAMWEAR

DW ®

'OUR DREAM IS BORN OUT OF DESIRE. POWERED BY BELIEF. ACHIEVED BY
ACTION. WHICH RESULTS IN SUCCESS. THIS IS THE IDEOLOGY BEHIND
DREAMWEAR.' A REPRESENTATION OF AMBITIOUS DREAMERS.

Vixen & Fox
Sydney, Australia
branding + website

vixenandfox.com.au

VIXEN&FOX

EST. 2013   SYDNEY

THE VIXEN&FOX PHILOSOPHY

Vixen & Fox
'Summer Siesta'
print pattern design

Vixen & Fox
'Chakra Shuttle'
print pattern design

**Vixen & Fox
'Blossoming Buds'**
print pattern design

**Vixen & Fox
'Toucan Tea Party'**
print pattern design

PLAY IT LIKE YOU MEAN IT

I love watching live music and seeing stories unfold on stage.
Each night is different and carves a different memory. Not every
performance will be perfect, but some acts are so captivating
that you have to see them every time they come to town.

There was one such band that I saw six times in one year.
I started calling them my local football team, I saw them
so often.

Their magnetism lay in the fact that they gave their all every single
night. Each performance had the energy and passion they would
have given their last ever show. Their attitude to their craft made
each moment memorable.

Obviously, designers are not, and probably never will be, rock
stars. But that shouldn't stop them having that same attitude.
Creative work should do what rock 'n' roll can: bring people
together, inspire them and make them want to take action.
It should come from the heart and a belief that you can
change the world around you.

When you ask yourself why you're doing your thing, take
the answer and multiply it by ten, by hundred or even more.

It will make for a memorable performance regardless of what you
do. Excitement, passion and good energy are contagious. Your
clients will keep coming back for more repeat performances.

Vixen & Fox
Sydney, Australia
typographic
print pattern

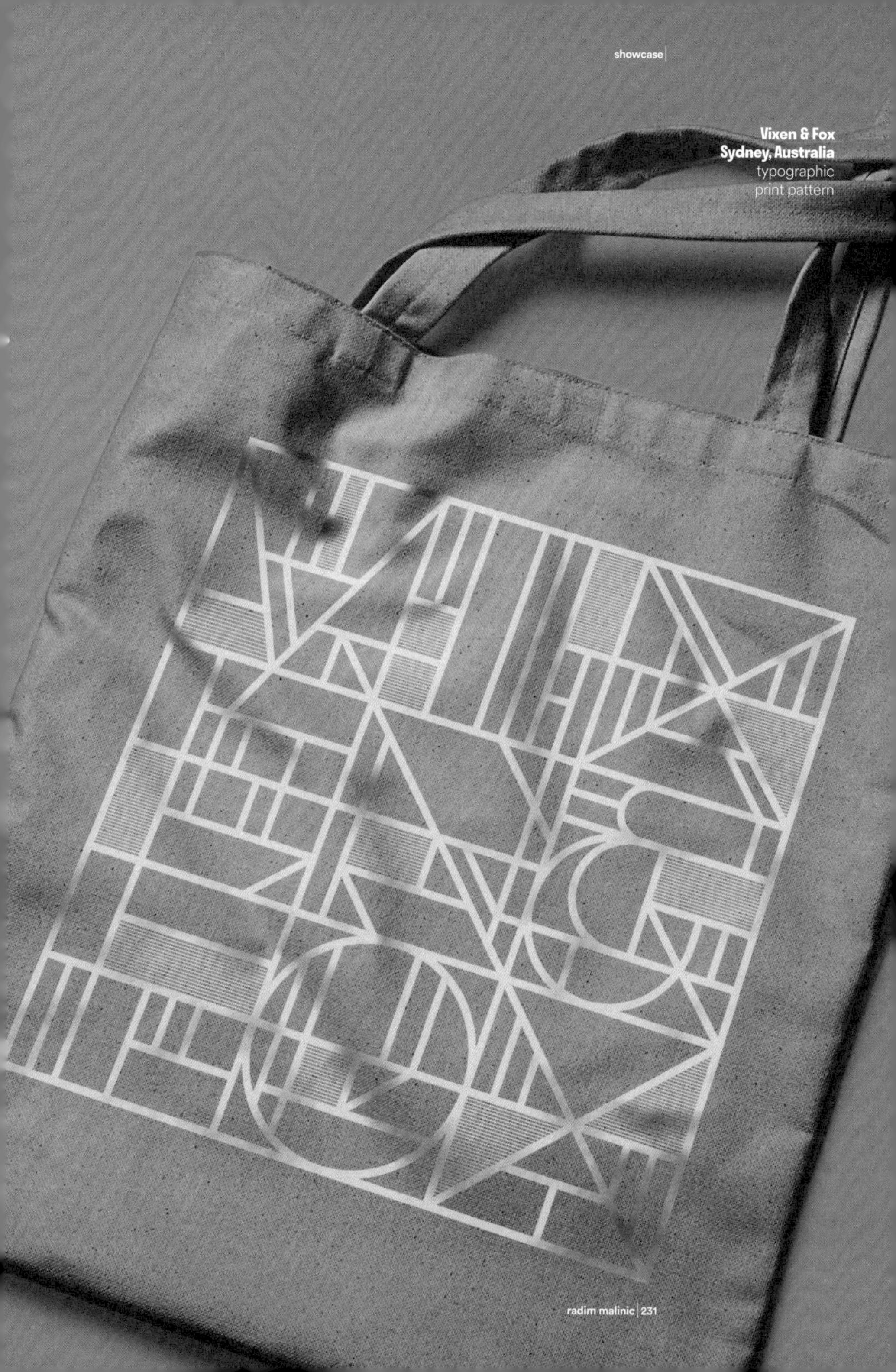

GROW AS A PERSON

I never thought I would have anything in common with loudmouth chef Gordon Ramsey, but it turns out that I do. During one of his shows, he paused from turning the air blue in his quest to save ailing eateries, and said something along the lines of: "Move to another country, learn the language, meet new people and follow your passion - you will grow as a person." Those words resonated with me. As it turns out, this is exactly what I did at the turn of the millennium.

I was born in the Czech Republic and, although I travelled around Europe a lot as a child with my family, this was the time to discover another country by myself. My passion was music, and this was one of the main reasons why I travelled to England. I wanted to be closer to the place that seemed to invent a new genre of music in a lunch break. I didn't have any plans, I was just a kid who was ready for whatever might come his way.

At first, music served as the connection with people I met. England was a whole new place where you could chat to almost anyone about grindcore, death metal, jazz, and soul until the early hours. I was naturally intrigued by all the idioms and colloquialisms of the English language. And sooner or later, graphic design became a topic of late-night conversations.

When my newfound passion for design turned into a career, it helped me to meet a huge number of inspiring people. Their knowledge is what inspired me to grow as a creative professional. Their passion for life is what inspired me to grow as a person. These experiences have shaped my life.

I can only repeat what the seldom philosophical chef once said - travel, discover, learn and make. You will never know what you might become tomorrow.

BRAND NU™ / ORIGINAL ARTWORK SERIES / DESIGNED & PRODUCED IN ENGLAND

REWIRE YOUR BRAIN

"The client hates it!" Ever had that feedback? It's possibly backed up by a rather baffling explanation. "The client hates yellow and brown next to each other!"

But who are these people with such strong opinions on these colours, carefully chosen to fit the rest of the campaign? How can there be such hostility towards a colour, image, illustration or typeface?

The problem is that 'hate' is a word hijacked for the purpose of lazy, unhelpful feedback. It happens everywhere: the singing TV car insurance man might be annoying, but surely not enough to really hate him. I could easily fill all the pages of this book just with things people 'hate' about every new version of iPhone iOS.

The word hate is convenient, but more often than not it's just a way to deal with new or uncomfortable situations.

Exciting things weren't built with vanilla. But today people 'hate' far too easily, and the word's overuse distracts us from thinking neutrally. Over time, all this negativity can impact your mood and your mind.

Rewire your brain and be brave. Don't get knocked by the haters. And don't be one yourself.

EVERY MISTAKE IS AN OPPORTUNITY

Mistakes get a bad rap. We have been led to believe
that only the correct way is appropriate, and it can seem
very black and white.

Of course, some mistakes can be costly and cause a lot of
headaches, but most of them are just an unexpected turn of
events during the creative process without huge implications.
It goes without saying that I'm not talking about the kind of errors
that cost lives, but most of the time a mishap, mistake
or whatever you'd like to name it as an opportunity to act,
and discover something new.

It's tempting to stick to tried-and-tested routes, but repetition
doesn't help your evolution. It keeps you stagnant. Repetition
should get a bad rap. Safe is boring for everyone. That's why
being curious, explorative, disruptive and innovative are the
brilliant side-effects of error. Cornflakes, antibiotics, microwave
ovens and potato chips are just some of the things that initially
arrived accidentally.

When you keep learning by play, any mistake is an opportunity to
help you grow. Nothing will or should be perfect all the time.

When you take a wrong turn you might end up travelling a bit
longer to your destination, but you can learn along the way.
Mistakes will always be the beginning of something new.

Enamel badges
for November Universe
product design

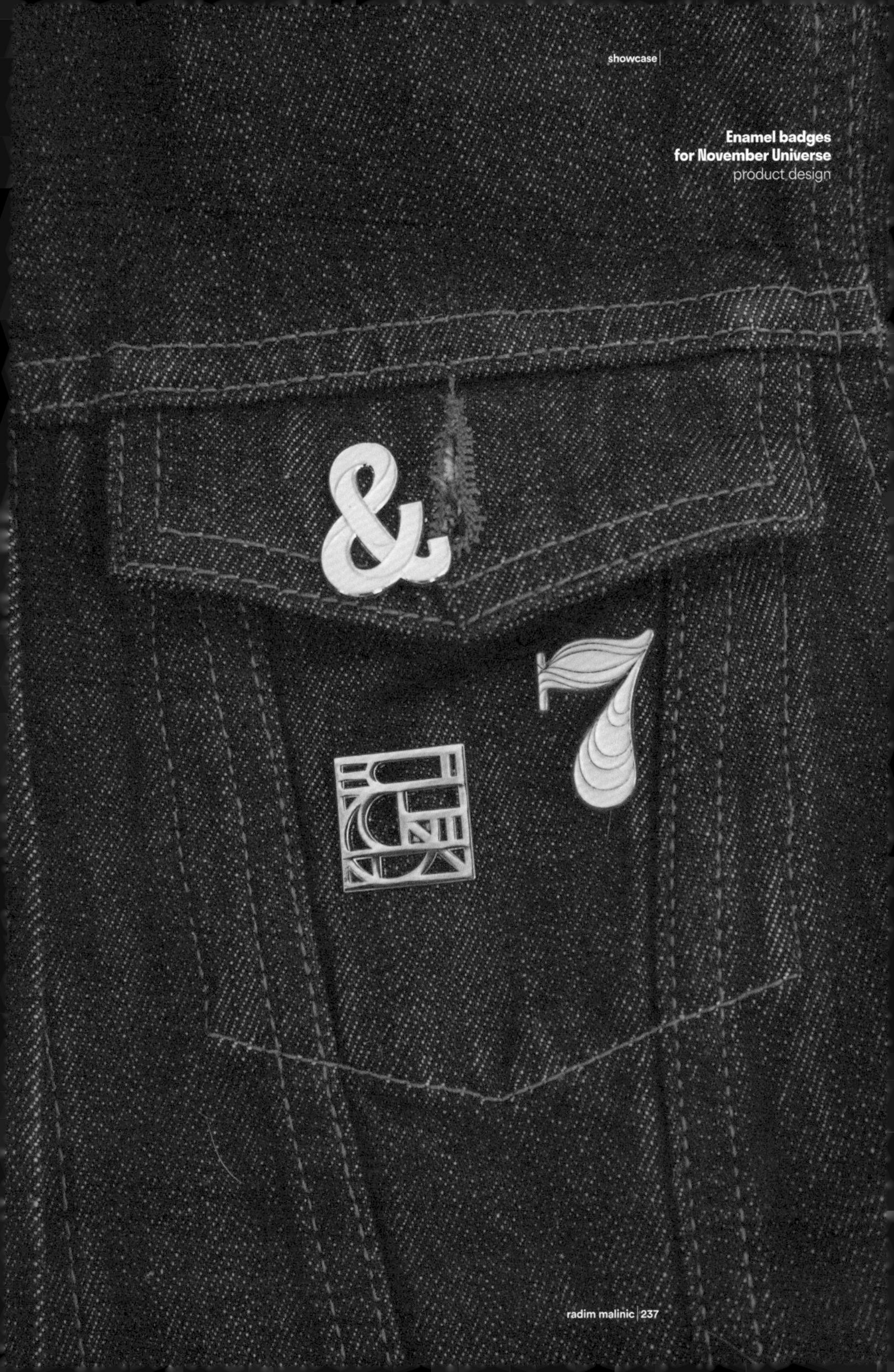

CLARITY versus FOG

Do you think you could cut out social media for a month or two? It's hard to realise how embedded it is in your life until you step away.

When you stop constantly checking the lives of others, you begin to observe your own thought patterns and see how idly scrolling Twitter feeds has become an autopilot setting. There are the jokes you think of tweeting, weird situations in the supermarket you have the urge to share on Facebook and an itching to take a photo of absolutely anything inane, knowing it will look irresistible through an Instagram filter. And that's just when you're sober.

Sociological studies have proven that using social media can make you feel depressed - a problem that simply didn't exist just a decade and a half ago. Curated lives are making people feel sad. Everyone tells us to follow. Nobody tells us to lead.

I've tried this experiment for two months. It took me about two weeks of social media separation before I stopped thinking in tweets and statuses. Not every thought is worthy of a spoken sentence, let alone a tweet. When your phone stays in your pocket for much longer periods of time, you might not have a picture to prove you've been to a hot new burger joint, but you will have a far sharper mind. Your productivity will improve, and you'll soon start seeing a clearing in the information fog.

We're so tied up in other people's newsfeeds, we can sometimes lose sight of our own thoughts. Fog is fun once in a while, but clarity wins.

'And that day
dust turned into gold'
typographic poster design

EVERYTHING IS A WORK IN PROGRESS

Anything created today can be improved tomorrow
or the next day. Everything that already exists does so as
its current version. Nothing is truly perfect, it's a work
in progress.

Instead of keeping focused on ourselves, we tend
to look around to see how everyone else is doing.
A comparison is the thief of joy.

There's no need to liken yourself to anyone else. There
will always be someone just a bit better, quicker, funnier
or more talented. There's no need to keep analysing the
differences. Maybe those people think exactly the same
about you. You never know.

However, nobody else is living your story. Keep exploring
and enjoying every day. We can think we will only stop
when we achieve perfection. But perfection can be boring:
a flawless object doesn't leave much room for imagination.
It's the problems in things that make your imagination
run wild. Those problems will keep you awake at night
and rightfully so. They are the driving force to keep
us going.

Look at your work and take a moment to think about your
next step. Whether it's a small move or a giant leap, you
are in charge. Look ahead and do your thing. This is your
own story.

EVERYTHING IS A WORK IN PROGRESS

BRAND-NU™ / ORIGINAL ARTWORK SERIES / DESIGNED & PRODUCED IN ENGLAND

ON NOT SEARCHING FOR HAPPINESS

When I was in my early twenties I was asked what I wanted to be in life. I didn't have an answer. I'd toyed with lots of different ideas, but I knew none of them were going to be my career. So I said that I wanted to be happy. In a swift reply that followed I was told that nobody gets paid for just being happy. Obviously.

Some months later, I stumbled into the world of graphic design and I realised that I could have found my answer. I was beginning to make steps in a new direction. However, I was still trying too hard to find that elusive happiness.

It was such an easy mistake to make. How often do we hear that we're collectively less happy than the generation before us, or the one before that? It's easy to buy into the belief that we have to be happy no matter what we do. Maybe we've become so preoccupied with measuring our personal happiness that we're driving ourselves into an unhappy cul-de-sac.

One way round the situation is to concentrate on living your own life and finding enjoyable work. Fully focussing on a creative project has been shown to boost serotonin levels. But at that moment when you're delivering a project of whatever size, you're more likely to feel anxious than chipper.

Once the task is over and you see what you've created, the struggle feels worth it. When you welcome the daily obstacles and focus on conquering them, moments of joy will appear. Instead of dreading the next project, you actually can't wait to get started again. You are enjoying your work.

When I wake up every morning, I realise how lucky I was to find this career. It's not easy, but it's always worth it. Now, I get paid for being happy.

'Go forth'
for Any Forty charity exhbition
digital illustration

GO FORTH ONTO THE NEVER ENDING PATH

AnyForty
x
Brand_Nu

THE IMPORTANCE OF MEANING

Like many other tech companies, music streaming service Spotify also gives its users an annual report full of data from their year in music.

From my report, I learned that I listened to 6,215 individual songs in a single year. That works out at about sixteen new tracks every day. But if you asked me what I could remember, I'd be hard-pushed to name my top ten albums from the year, let alone songs. Today, music is everywhere: you don't have to hunt down special releases like previous generations did.

The world of visual creativity is similar. Galleries are no longer the only places you can see art - it's accessible to everyone. Images are everywhere: Instagram and Pinterest alone house billions of images. Just like the music we hear, the majority of what we see gets quickly forgotten.

It's easy to discover something new, but it is so much harder to make it stay in our lives for long enough to be remembered.

When we provide people with the option to connect with our work, let's try to put a meaning in our art. Now that you can get instant feedback, it's tempting to put something out almost daily for the world to see. But it's work with a wider message that will have a lasting connection with people. Those are the pieces that will remain in your folio and people's memories.

Meaningful work created for the right reasons will never age badly.

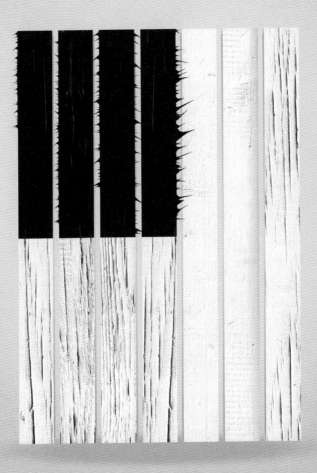

KICKING OUT SELF-DOUBT

Why does confidence sometimes feel so fleeting?
And why does it do a runner when we most need it?

You could be working on a huge project where everything is at stake. You don't doubt a thing, and your confidence is working its magic on the client. You think about solutions, but they worry about potential problems.

Then something switches and a wave of disruptive thoughts and emotions come to the forefront of your mind. Things don't feel like they're on your side any more. You start analysing every tiny detail, and making simple choices feels impossible.

We worry about putting ourselves and our work out there for public scrutiny. So many ideas never came to fruition for fear of failure. Why should we care about what people think?

Kicking out self-doubt is just about giving it a go and putting yourself in a noise-cancelling zone. It's about forgetting about what others might say.

Focus on the end result and forget about everything else. It makes the future battles just a little bit easier to win. Once you get started, just keep going. Not every project is destined to be the most pivotal in your career, but each is important for your progress. Every start you make is a step towards your end goal. If others can do it, so can you. Kick out your self-doubt.

A SMART WATCH ISN'T THE ANSWER

The life of a 21st-century freelancer can be adventurous, but it also involves a lot of sitting at a desk. In the creative industry, office hours can be a lot longer than nine to five, which means even more sedentary time.

We sit down so much that Apple has implemented a special function into its smartwatch to tell you it's time to get up and move a bit. We've somehow become a species that needs reminding to do something so natural, as we sit about damaging our health.

Although a smartwatch tries its best to take care of our health, we need much more than a few minutes of airplane-style exercise to help us think and work better.

I decided to get a dog instead of a smartwatch. Through having a dog, I've rediscovered my passion for the outdoors and for running. I have an excuse to take long lunchtime walks or morning runs in the most interesting places. Although, for a while, I became that person posting daily photos of my dog to Instagram...

My advice is you don't need a smartwatch, you need a dog. It changed my life and it will change yours. I don't get a ping on my wrist, I get a tug of my trousers to remind me it's time to go and leave the full inbox of unanswered emails for a little bit longer.

It can be a struggle on deadline day and training a puppy can test your patience, but it's worth it. My dog Hendrix is my fitness trainer, resident comedian and all-round fun numpty who makes me smile every day.

Hendrix

ABOUT
THE AUTHOR

Radim Malinic is a creative director and designer living and working in South West London. He runs Brand Nu® an award winning studio. Taking a multidisciplinary approach, he works across creative direction, design, illustration, typography, product design and music video direction to form a practice based around positivity, message and meaning.

Before finding his calling in the creative industry, Czech born Malinic was an ice hockey player, a bassist in death metal bands, an indie DJ, music journalist and student of Economics and Business management. At the break of the new millennium, Malinic moved to the UK to explore the expansive music scene, only to find even an greater interest in art and graphic design. Since then his eclectic interests have seen him working with some of the biggest brands, companies and bands in the world. Clients include Harry Potter, London Film Museum, SyCo, Sprite, WWF and USAID amongst many others. Whatever the project, Radim's central belief is to help his clients achieve their objective by delivering the best work possible.

Aside from his studio work, Radim designs products for his brand 'November Universe', releases music and tours design events and universities globally with his talks and lectures designed to inspire and support self-development in the creative industry.

In March 2016, Malinic released his publication, Book of Ideas. The Amazon #1 Graphic Arts bestseller has helped novices and professionals across the world to find a new way of approaching their creative work.

Radim was born in 1978 in Frydek-Mistek in the Czech Republic, and has been based in the United Kingdom since 2000.

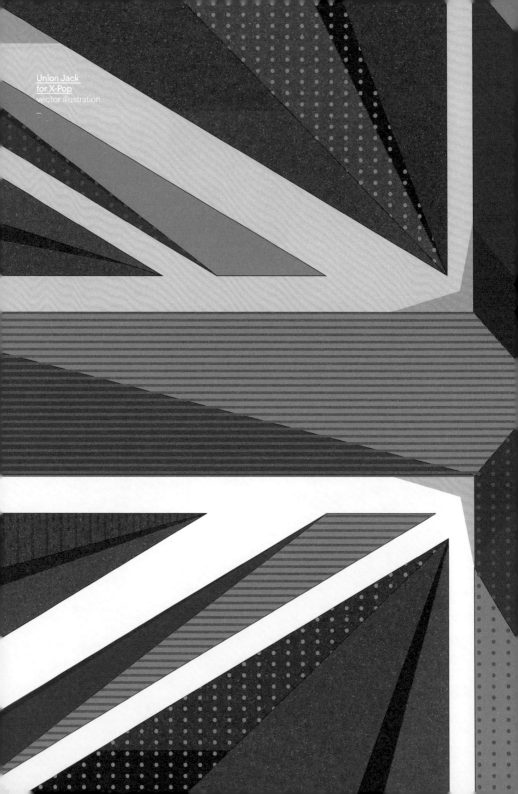

Union Jack
for X-Pop
vector illustration
_

THANKS AND ACKNOWLEDGEMENTS

I am eternally thankful to have met so many people who have played a part in my career and life. The people listed here have had an impact on my practice, inspired and pushed me to create better work, given me a leg up in the world, pushed me in the right direction, hung out at conferences around the world or shared a cold beer closer to home, are clients who became friends or are friends who became collaborators. They are future superstars!

Daniel Clark, Francois Hoang, Thi Hoang, Gordon Reid, Luke Whitaker, Mark Ford, John Deane, Jonathan Sands, Leslie Hardcastle, Linda Ayton, Thorsten Klein, Greg Browne, Nathalie Gordon, Rahul Bhatt, Wayne Johns, Aaron Phipps, Katie Lang, Bikie Isharaza and Debs Isharaza, Alex Suchet, Chris Page, Charlie Sells, Chelsie Sixsmith, Soy Mustafa, James Collingwood, Johan Lindh, Hanna Nilsson, Emma Axling, Daniel Nelson, Kyle Wilkinson, Daniel Maw, Aaron Draplin, James White, Chuck Anderson, Gwen O'Brien, Julien Vallée, Michael Cina, Rizon Parein, Craig Minchington, Billy Bogiatzoglou, Rik Oostenbroek, Peter Jaworowski, Marcin Molski, Saad Moosajee, Lizzy Mary Cullen, Cameron Duthie, Paul Skeffington, Seb Lester, Johann Chan, Neil Bennett, Tony Harmer, Mariah Anden, Fabien Barral, Hector Ayuso, Natalie Koutia, Ellen Hancock, Ash Thorpe, Stefan Sagmeister, David Nuff, Phoebe Ellis, Ben Edwards, Tom Muller, Dines & Blup, Franz Jeitz, Fabio Sasso, Mike Harrison, Pete Harrison, Luke Freeman, Adhemas Batista, Jonathan Ball, David Delin, Ade Mills, Steven Bonner, Kerry Roper, Andy Potts, Shawn Pucknell, Jac Poole, Alfred Park, Karoly Kiralyfalvi, Bram Timmer, Krysta Youngs, Bea MK, Harry Roberts, Gavin Strange, Alan Wardle, Naomi Atkinson, Alex Mathers, George Smerin, Alex Donne-Johnsson, Nic Yeeles, Loic Sattler, Maciej Hajnrich, David Stephen, Peter Appleton, Toby Vane, Stephen McCleery, Lucy Kitchen, Mark Cooper, Lloyd Evans, Thain Lurk, Antony Kitson, Mark Best, David Carson, Sam Gilbey, Anna Mullin, Matt MacQuarrie, Paul Ridney, David Stypka, Radim Houfek, Jonny Greene, Che McPherson, Chris Alexander, Mr Bingo, Gmunk, Liam Miller, Dominic Wilcox, Emily Gosling and Anne Wollenberg

The biggest shouts go to Philip Goodeve-Docker who dedicated his life trying to make a difference in the world. A true legend!

Thanks to my family Sandra, Laura, Eva & Ellie.

The most wholehearted thanks and love go to
Rachel Bloodworth for all her endurance and patience,
and for helping to make me who I am today.

This book is dedicated to Harper Lux Freda.